Peter Sager

The technological Gap between the superpowers

Published by the Swiss Eastern
Institute Press

Contents

APPENDIX

The technological gap as seen in a comparison of Soviet and U. S. industrial branches.

Original title: «Die technologische Lücke zwischen Ost und West»
(Verlag SOI, Bern 1971. ISBN 3 85913 051 X).
Translated from the German by Claude Rieser.
© 1972 by Swiss Eastern Institute Ltd. Berne
Steiger Druck AG Bern
ISBN 3 85913 057 9

I. The Soviet economic status

On December 15, 1969, the Plenum of the Central Comittee of the Communist Party of the Soviet Union discussed the state of the national economy. The report presented to the participating members was grim. In spite of the fact that information on that meeting has been scarce, the wave of criticism aimed at the existing economic situation has not yet abated. The results of the Plenum have been widely discussed at all levels of the Party, of the Komsomol, and of the Soviet trade unions. During the first three months of 1970, the Soviet press has been filled with statements of resolution in tune with Brezhnev's estimation of the economic situation. While these criticize the serious failures in the execution of the Plan, the press promises its assistance to correct them. The «Ekonomiche-skaya Gazeta» (April 1970) has concisely and clearly listed the deficiencies: «The Plenum has soundly and extensively analyzed the condition, as well as the development, of our economy and of the political and organizational work of the Party in the current phase of the building of Communism. It has examined the provisional results of the State's and the Party's activity during the past years, as well as some of the problems linked with the elaboration of future Plans. Serious errors have cropped up in our economic development and in its practical management which prevent a maximum use of the reserves available to Socialist economy. The diminishing rate of growth in several branches of the industry, coupled with the slow increase of work productivity and production volume, have been duly noted at the Central Committee Plenum.»

The day after this session of the Central Committee, W. F. Garbusov, Minister of Finance, in his budget speech to the Supreme Soviet of the USSR, also dealt with the nation's economic problems. His exposé can be summarized as follows: work productivity grows more slowly than the average salary.

The overall picture presented by the central administration remains somewhat blurred and lacks detailing, but it gives a true indication of the present state of the economy in the Soviet Union.

The steel industry did not reach the quantitative result forecast in the Plan; in December 1970 alone, the production of extracted ore was one million tons short, a deficiency which led to the accumulative difficulties known to have plagued the subordinated industries («Pravda,» January 22, 1970). The quality of metallurgical products has been severely critized (Ekonomicheskaya Gazeta, September 1969): raw steel, sheet steel, and, most of all, steel tubing — which is of such inferior quality that it often cannot be electrowelded. These shortcomings have been attributed to the inferior and outdated mechanical equipment in the factories.

There are also many signs of trouble in the chemical industry. The October 1968 issue of «Voprosy ekonomiki» points out that six of the chemical plants imported from the West employ eight times more workers than similar Western enterprises.

The goal set by the Plan for the production of timber has not been reached. All in all, only a fifth of the wood for felling can be found in Russia's western industrial regions. Yet 70 % of the total output is industrially processed there, and 30 % only in the whole of Siberia. This requires the transportation to the western regions of about half the Russian timber, a process which involves sizeable problems and price increases. The cost of transportation can sometimes double, if not triple, the sale price of timber.

Similarly, agricultural production has not lived up to Soviet expectations. Worth 79 billion rubles, the gross output was 2,5 % lower than last year's, while, according to the Plan, it should have been 5 % higher. This retrogression is doubly important since great efforts to increase production have been made in the last few years. It is significant that, contrary to common pratice, no yearly figures were given for the production of wheat. In this context, the Czechoslovak Minister of Foreign Trade, F. Hamouz, has made the following comment about the problems facing the Soviets in their corn deliveries (as reported in the «Prager Volkszeitung» of July 11, 1969): «Due to damages caused by the inclemency of the weather, millions of acres of seeded fields had to be plowed all over again this year (1969), and many millions more which had not yet been harvested were covered with snow.»

The Soviet press attributes the alarming state of the national economy to shortcomings in four different fields: production, work productivity, operational profits, and national income. According to «Pravda» of January 25, 1970, the industrial production increase is of 7 %, instead of the 7.3 % predicted by the Plan («Pravda», December 14, 1968); the operational profits have increased by 10 % instead of 14.1 %, the national income by 6 % instead of 6.5 %, the industrial work productivity by 4.8 % instead of 5.9 %, the building trade by 3 % instead of 6.5 %.

The Soviets were especially counting on an increase in work productivity to set their economy on an upward trend. According to «Pravda» of Dezember 11, 1968, the director of the Plan and Vice-minister, Dikolai Baibakov, had clearly indicated that such was their goal. Therein lies one of the main chronic problems affecting the Communist economy. The will to work, paralyzed by the System, leads to a lack of discipline and a wasteful labor policy. The paralyzing effect of the System is also a factor which contributes, albeit not exclusively, to the continual decrease of the Russian birthrate during the last decade: 17.8 % to 9.8 % (1967); this phenomenon has had adverse effects, particularly in Eastern Siberia, even on a political level.

Investments, amounting to 70.5 billion rubles, are 2.7 % behind the Plan's prediction. As usual, heavy industry takes the lion's share with 86.3 % of all new investments, leaving a percentage of only 13.7 to light industry. And since heavy industry is still contributing primarily to the increase of Soviet power rather than to the benefit of the Soviet consumer, its burden on the Russian population is not to be lifted in the foreseeable future.

In several recent speeches, Brezhnev has hinted at the shadows darkening the Soviet economy; he is witnessing the close of a decade which started full of hopes with Khrushchev, but ended riddled with disappointments.

The contrast is obvious. In 1960, the Soviet Union was at the vanguard of space-travel. Only three years after the Soviets had successfully launched their first artificial satellite, Gagarin's flight astounded the world. Less than ten years later, Armstrong planted the star-spangled banner on the moon while Luna 15 crashed abortively.

In 1960, the Soviet thought that their economic overtaking of the United States was near at hand. Khrushchev had predicted it for 1970; he had even indicated that 1980 would mark the beginning of integral communism. And yet, as the alloted time to the deadline grew shorter, the Russian leader's prediction gradually turned into a vanishing and always receding mirage. Nowadays, economists such as Sakharov, Kapitsa, and Medvedev, not to mention a number of writers and artists, emphatically point out that the dictatorship which brought about a fast, if costly, industrialization has now become an obstacle to greater development.

If, in the early Sixties, the Soviets could still hope to have subdued what they thought was an erratic phenomenon when they smashed down the Hungarian freedom uprising, they found out differently in the spring of 1968 in Czechoslovakia. In 1960, Moscow still expected Red Chinese and Soviet views to basically coincide; in 1969, open warfare broke out between the two countries, on the Ussuri border.

The year 1964 saw the fall of Nikita Khrushchev, the leader who had seemed determined to break away from political dogmatism and intolerance, and who appeared anxious to cautiously and gradually promote an opportunity for contacts with the West. But this trend reached a point where it threatened to become irreversible: it was thus essentially responsible for Khrushchev's political demise.

And so the Soviet workaday routine has become darker. However, are the aforementioned facts and figures sufficient to indicate that the Plan has partially failed? If, out of ambition and as an incentive to work harder, the Plan's goals were set exceedingly high, then even a partial execution can be considered as a performance above average. The Soviet economic plans were underestimated in the West when they were introduced in 1928.

The aforementioned comparisons between the early and the late sixties can be considered as significant symptoms of the less than satisfactory economic picture in the Soviet Union. So fare as domestic policies are concerned, the restalinization trend is making more progress than the economic situation. The foreign policy gains are but a meager consolation, even though the Soviet Union has many irons in the fire. But the increase of its influence in the Near East has cost Moscow more than it can afford: the Soviet productive power is in the process of being overworked.

What does the situation look like at present? The answer is of great import for the years to come: during the forthcoming decade, the Soviet Union will have to cross the border which indicates either the beginning of the end of Communism, or the end of the Socialist beginning. In 1980, it should be a lot easier to tell whether the gigantic experiment initiated 50 years ago by Lenin is on its supposedly irresistible way to victory — or to its downfall.

The outcome will greatly depend upon the economic output and on its development, these two factors being themselves decisively influenced by the objective and subjective ability to remain at the vanguard of technology, and by the capacity to satisfy the requirements of what is already known as the technotronic age.

Once we become better acquainted with the nature, the scale, and the future development of the technological gap between the superpowers, we shall be able to come forth with opinions and evaluations (our findings cannot be of a categorical nature) based on a stronger foundation.

This, however, requires comparing what is not comparable. The statistical data in Communist countries are not only fragmentary, but also compiled according to criteria which differ from Western ones. Market-prices with individual cost and production allowances which permit value comparisons between different products (pears and apples, for example) are not available. In our era of rapid technological progress, there is no possibility of assessing the growth of work productivity in a given country over a long period of time.

In a remarkable series of articles in the «Neue Zürcher Zeitung» (published separately in the NZZ collection «Schriften zur Zeit», no. 6), Christian Lutz has explained how difficult it is to analyze the technological gap between the United States and Western Europe. Yet these areas are much more comparable to one another than either is to the Soviet Union.

In attempting to analyze the technological gap between East and West, only the few quantitative figures which are available will be used for the purpose of interpreting their implication in a wider context. A different method will be used in the appendix for a comparative study of the situation and the development of several Soviet and U.S industrial branches, made on the basis of written testimonies and oral reports. If allowance is made for individual approaches, an objective appraisal of the facts should be possible.

II. The technological development

Here now is a brief outline of the development of Soviet technology. The term «technology» represents, in this context, the whole of the methods, techniques, and processes by which raw materials are transformed into finished products. There is technological progress when new methods, techniques, or processes make the following possible:
- a cost decrease through savings in factors of production, work, capital, real estate, and enterprise;
- an increase in the quality of finished products;
- the manufacture of new products.

Technological progress does not simply indicate the introduction of the assembly line, the utilization of machinery, or the change-over to a more economical mass production system, but also the inclusion of advanced methods of operation (such as statistical quality control, automation) and management.

In 1917, when the Bolshevist Party captured control over Russia, then an agrarian and industrially backward state, Lenin still believed and hoped that a successful German revolution could be the spearhead of the Communist movement. His expectation did not materialize. The revolution failed to spread to other parts of Europe and the Soviet Union only had herself to depend on. In 1921, Lenin changed course with his introduction of a new economic policy. He liberalized the national economy far more than the reform proposals, which have appeared since then, ever attempted to do. He began to develop foreign trade with «capitalist» countries. Full priority was given to the development of heavy industry to the detriment of light industry and its production of consumer goods.

Thus the Soviet Union tried to keep pace with worldwide technological development, using every available means. Imports of machinery and equipment supplied the Russians with Western technical know-how. From 1923 to 1932, imports quintupled and the change-over to industrialization came about at a frantic pace.

Industrialization was indeed Soviet economy's only oustanding achievement. A detailed survey by Anthony C. Sutton (Western Technology and Soviet Economic Development: 1917 to 1930, Stanford 1968) points out that Western technical aid was mainly responsible for this spectacular evolution: 95 % of the Soviet industrial structure benefited from it.

In 1928, Stalin, who meanwhile had won the battle for the succession, introduced the Five-Year Plan. In 1932, at the end of its initial period of enforcement began an era of isolation, characterized by a tendency to self-sufficiency which lasted until 1951.

But this isolation proved to be a disadvantage — and not only when the Soviet-Union found itself involved in the last World War and lost contact with the technological development in the rest of the world. A few years before his death, Stalin himself altered the course of Soviet politics. The resumption of a coexistence policy, a concept introduced by Lenin in 1921, contributed to an increase in foreign trade which in turn facilitated the import by the Russians of badly needed equipment and mechanical installations.

The Soviet Union also uses other means to obtain the technical know-how required, one of which, commercial intelligence, is not the least productive. Many a nuclear spy, for example, must have spared Moscow considerable development expenditure.

Furthermore, many patents and foreign licenses have been purchased, agreements have been signed with foreign companies and business groups for the purpose of exchanging scientific and technical data. And, above all, foreign trade literature in science and technical subjects has been closely and regularly studied by the Russians.

Within the scope of the Soviet Academy of Sciences, an institute employs several thousand full-time or part-time employees, translators, and scientific writers. In 1960, about ten thousand trade magazines and periodicals were scanned by its members; today, more than fifteen thousand are examined every year. Among them, more than five thousand are of Western origin; they are reported on every year. All in all, the institute supplies yearly more than half million digests and provides the results of its investigations to the specialists concerned. Several years ago, a high-ranking representative of the Swiss Railroads taking part in a Moscow conference was surprised at how well informed his hosts were on tests which had taken place in Switzerland, a few weeks before, on a new, electrically heated, steam engine.

Moreover, the Soviet Union receives substantial help, which in some cases can be very extensive, from the scientific and technical exchange program elaborated with the United States. Moscow's readiness to sign the renunciation of force agreement with Bonn was mainly explained by its hope to sharply increase the importation of West-German technology — thanks to West-German credit if possible.

Finally, the Soviets have built up, mainly since 1950, a powerful technological potential replete with research and development facilities, in which Soviet inventions can be tested out, while foreign ones can be adapted to Russian use. However, if the sale of Soviet licenses and patents has been increasing, the number of Soviet inventions is still limited. One exception is the Soviet Union's power-oriented and strategically important heavy industry: in some branches of the military, such as the construction of large helicopters, the Soviet Union appears to be ahead of Western powers.

A country's economic potential depends on the number of its wage-earners. The latter hinges on two factors: the size of the population and its percentage of wage-earners. The age-structure of the population and the manpower drain are essential aspects which here have to be left out of consideration.

Economic potential also depends on the productivity of the wage-earners. Work productivity varies not only according to work discipline, but also according to the type and the quantity of invested capital (machinery and factory installations), and to the level of technical development.

It should be emphasized once again how difficult it is not only to estimate the average technological level of a country, but, most of all, to compare it with that of another country, since reliable comparison standards are lacking.

Nevertheless, some figures are available. They bolster the general impression of a substantial Eastern decline in the East-West confrontation, a feeling which prevails among well-informed Western observers. These figures provide the following indications:

- gross national product per work and capital unit (factor productivity),

- gross national product per worker (work productivity),

- value of invested capital per worker.

Using two comparative studies, the first based on U. S. prices, the other on local prices, we can compile these figures on the basis of the writings of several authors, such as Abram Bergson's Planning and Productivity under Soviet Socialism (1968, p. 22). We thus obtain the following chart:

	Factor productivity	Work productivity	Value of invested capital per worker
U. S.	100	100	100
Northwestern Europe	55	48	45
Italy	35	33	31
U. S. S. R	34	30	31

These data are meager. The efforts of an entire research team and much time would be required to complement them. Still, the value of the figures obtained could only be extremely limited.

If we take the value of invested capital per worker as basis for our calculations, we should then be able to assume not only that the value of invested capital can be estimated with precision, but also that the whole of technology is included in that factor. It would imply a sort of «physical» and very limited definition of technology. Furthermore, the structure of the invested capital, as well as its output level, varies from country to country, from industry to industry, from enterprise to enterprise. This type of problem, encountered in establishing a comparative economic survey, is not limited to countries under Communist rule. For example, should the invested capital of Western enterprises be considered as rateable value, as nominal value of capital stock, or as stock market value?

Factor and work productivity are the expression of the general production level; the latter is related to elements other than technology, which concerns us most directly here, such as the relative differences in raw material wealth, in educational levels, and in management.

If one takes into consideration the differences in the quality of work potential (level of acquired know-how, degree of work discipline, utilization rate of reserve manpower among women, the aged, and the young), the productivity gap would probably decrease but without changing the trends.

11

Some Soviet data (Voprosy ekonomiki, October 1969) show, for example, that for every 100 skilled plant workers, there are four store-clerks in the U. S. and 50 in the Soviet Union. For each skilled worker, there are 38 unskilled U. S. workers, 85 Russian ones. Approximately 75 % of Soviet factories must manufacture 75 % of their own tools, instruments, and equipment themselves, either individually or in small series.

Even when one takes into account all possible restrictions, the differences in effectively utilized technology are still a major factor in the international differences in productivity. They show that the average level of technology in the Soviet economy is far below the U. S. average level, and considerably below Western Europe's. According to the aforementioned Soviet sources, in 1965 40,9 % of the Soviet industrial workers still had to work without the help of mechanical equipment.

It should be pointed out that the few figures quoted offer but an inadequate margin for product quality allowance, particularly in dealing with the Communist planned economy in which quality differences are not reflected in price differences since there is no market. The productivity gap would be even wider if the quality of finished products could be taken into consideration.

Actually, the results of our findings do not correspond with today's estimation — or, rather, over-estimation — of the Soviet economy which, until about 10 years ago, had been underestimated. This over-estimation evidently originates from the fact that an exaggerated import was attributed to isolated, albeit undeniably meritorious, achievements in Soviet production. The following statistics were published in «Kommunist» (November 1967) and «Pravda» (January 25, 1970).

	1950	1960	1969
Electricity (billion kWh)	91	292	689
Steel (million tons)	27	65	110
Mineral oil (million tons)	38	148	328
Coal (million tons)	261	510	608
Cement (million tons)	10	46	90
Tractors (×1000)	117	239	442
Textiles (billion meters)	5	8	9
Radio sets (×1000)	1072	4165	7300
TV sets (×1000)	12	1726	6600

While these figures certainly indicate that the Soviet Union is progressing on the road to industrialization, they do not reveal the price which has had to be paid for this succes, namely a consistently low living standard, nor do they disclose the expenditure which should be as closely proportional to the output as possible. But, above all, it is impossible to make any prediction whatsoever on the basis of the aforementioned figures.

III. The discontinued expansion

Of particular importance in estimating the technological gap and its possible development in the future are the technological rates of growth. These can show us — at least in the main — whether the gap between the Soviet Union and the industrialized West is growing greater or smaller. The comparison listed below indicates the average annual growth rates of productivity factors (coefficient of production per capital and work unit) for the Soviet Union, the U. S., and Western Europe during two different periods:

	1951—1960	1961—1967
U. S.	1.7	2.7
U. S. S. R.	2.8	1.3
	1955—1964	1960—1964
U. S.	2.0	3.0
Northwest Europe	3.2	3.0
Italy	4.4	4.5
U. S. S. R.	2.4	1.7

The aforementioned statistical reservations are valid here also; but these figures nevertheless have considerable importance in discerning tendencies. In the fifties, the productivity growth rate was greater in the Soviet Union than in the United States, whereas during the sixties, it was considerably smaller. The Soviet figures for the latter ten years seem to be far below those of Western Europe, particularly Italy and West

Germany. Even for the period between 1950–1964, the Soviet growth rate is lower than that of all West European countries, with the exception of Great Britain. The Soviet productivity growth rate from 1960 to 1964 is approximately half that of the West, including Great Britain and the United States.

Insofar as productivity development reflects a technological gap — and this is most often the case — we can now see that the technological gap between the Soviet Union and the U. S. became smaller during the fifties, and increased again during the sixties. Compared with Western Europe, the *relative* situation of the Soviet Union has been in constant deterioration since 1950. If we compare it with Italy — the production level of which was close to that of the Soviet Union at about the middle of the sixties — we find that is was precisely at that time that the *relative* deterioration of the Soviet situation was the highest.

This corroborates the comparison per decade made in the first chapter: it was at the end of the fifties that the Soviet Union could claim its greatest successes, and this was particularly striking in the field of space exploration. As Khrushchev announced with optimism, the Soviet Union then appeared on the way to catching up with the United States by 1970 and overtaking them by 1980. Ten years later, however, at the end of the sixties, these hopes had vanished. Striking successes had no longer been forthcoming; and self-criticism about Soviet economic problems was increasing to a degree hitherto unprecedented.

How can this phenomenon be explained? Since the end of the Second World War, the Soviet Union has participated in the technological revolution to a much lesser degree than Western Europe. As expected, Western Europe had made up the time lost during the war. At the end of the war, Soviet industry was more backward than that of Western Europe. Consequently, a similar progress at an even faster pace might have been expected. The gap did indeed begin to disappear during the 1950s, but it increased again later. It was as if the Soviet Union had suddenly become short of breath. Nor was this abrupt halt an unavoidable development; Japan, for example, appears to have escaped it. It is precisely this phenomenon which is in need of an explanation — even though it may only be provisional.

Both Communist and non-Communist economists agree that the low rate of Soviet production is a consequence of its low productivity. We believe this phenomenon to be a consequence of the economic system in the Soviet Union: on the one hand, management efficiency is chronically unsatisfactory, and on the other, the political organization condemns Soviet industry to the lowest possible yield. The people — workers and contractors — lack the necessary economic and moral incentives for greater efficiency. The state retains a relatively greater amount of the gross national product, and, for this purpose, it has to restrict the freedom of the citizen. This lack of incentives, both economic *and* moral, results in preventing the Soviet Union from breaking out of the vicious circle in which it is imprisoned.

Why, then, did the Soviet Union succeed in catching up with the West to such a large extent during the fifties? If low productivity is a consequence of the system, then we must look for an answer to this question in the political developments which took place during this period.

There were great political changes during that decade. The first of these was the death of Stalin in March 1953, marking the end of the period of open terror. The dictator's successors could not have made the situation worse, nor increased the terror. In one way or another, Stalin's death resulted in a natural liberalization, at least for a while. The forced labor camps started to empty and obvious forms of terror began to disappear. The general feeling of relief was an important moral stimulant for improved efficiency. Furthermore, important sales of gold to the West enabled Malenkov to obtain consumer goods which had not been included in the Plan, and which were thrown on the Soviet market to gain some loyalty from the population. The motive was political, but it nevertheless provided an economic stimulus. This change of climate was needed to widen a base of industrial progress which had been created largely by force. The successful launching of an artifical satellite would certainly have been possible had Stalin lived longer; but it would not have been the expression of a generally felt and widespread impetus.

Along with this new wave of optimism and goodwill came other changes. In June 1953, East German workers and youth had already tried to take advantage of the Kremlin's weakening leadership. But the repression of the uprising indicated that changes could not come about so quickly, as evidenced again by the Polish «spring». The violent repression of the Hungarian fight for freedom — starkly contrasting with the new expectations — could be explained at the time as a relapse, and as such, as an exception to the rule.

In the few years which followed Stalin's death, everything which had been previously thought or dreamed about against totalitarianism appeared to prevail. Pasternak's «Dr. Zhivago», Dudintsev's «Not by Bread Alone» were universally seen as lights from under a bushel. It was then that appeared many examples of the Russian creative genius: Solzhenitsyn, Terts (Sinyavsky), Arzhak (Daniel), and many others. It was a soaring of the spirit which could have been the incentive for everyone to work harder and better.

But the future was not to hold to the promise of these years. The improvement in the Soviet climate during the 1950s did not continue. Unfortunately, the Russian improvement of the fifties was only noticed in the West when the sixties were well under way; and the readiness for dialogue and contact which would have been so fruitful a few years earlier then fell on barren ground. The Soviet regime realized that it was paying a heavy political price for the greater liberty which made an improved economic performance possible. Its hold on the people was growing weaker. Greater economic liberty was an incentive to better discipline at the factory bench — but to extend that liberty to the political sphere, which was inevitable, would lead to an end of political discipline.

Khrushchev, whose personality was remarkable among dictators, was unable to find a viable compromise. A man of excessive spontaneity, he believed in limits of tolerance which were too far apart. He switched too quickly from one extreme to the other. If he was partly the man of peaceful coexistence, he was also the man of brutal struggle for power, who, during the Cuban crisis in autumn 1962, tried to overpower the United States. He was not only the man who recommended Western economic methods to his own people, but also the man who, in 1962, brought out regulations which were designed to greatly increase the power of the Communist Party over the economy.

Such wide oscillations were fraught with risk — particularly since any development, if it lasts long enough, acquires its own momentum, begins to be hard to control, and becomes irreversible. A continuation of the evolution which took place during these few years of Soviet creativity in the middle Fifties would have led to a situation within Russia of the kind now known as the Prague «spring» — with the very important difference that Eastern Europe would not have been able to intervene in the Soviet Union as the Soviet Union intervened in Czechoslovakia in 1968.

So another change of climate, this time toward a «restalinization», became manifest in the Soviet Union. It had already started before the fall Khrushchev, just as a very meek liberalization attempt was initiated ten years earlier, before Stalin's death (peaceful coexistence, readiness to establish trade links with the West).

Contrasting with the relatively relaxed regulations existing under Khrushchev, the new work law adopted by the 8th Supreme Soviet (Pravda, July 17, 1970) requires the worker's unconditional subordination to the management, so that «Socialist work discipline» can be more effectively enforced. Violations of this discipline will be more severely punished; judges and public prosecutors have been specifically instructed to that effect.

We believe that these changes in the political climate are directly linked to the variations in economic growth which have been analyzed. If so, several important considerations can be brought forth.

Improvements in the political climate, even when they are the indispensable conditions for greater economic growth, are much too dangerous for any Communist regime. The Communist Party, and the government which issues from it, will sign their own death warrant if, as the Prague reformers were ready to do, they accept the full political consequences. In this case — and only in this case — it would be a renunciation of the ideal of world revolution, of the communization of the world and of the aspiration to universal domination. What would be left would be a creation so totally different in essence and quality that it could no longer be called — in any traditional sense — a Communist regime. It would be a regime which could quite normally insert itself in the wide spectrum of Western states.

However, if a development in which East and West converge is only possible through a complete change in the essence of the Communist regime, we can assume that a real convergence of the two systems is impossible. Only the victory of either one of the two systems is possible.

Thus, Soviet economic productivity will always lag behind that of the West, as long as the Communist system does not succeed in creating a new type of man who will work as automatically as a robot — which appears unthinkable — and as long as the Western system does not destroy itself — which has now unhappily become imaginable. This assertion of the long-term lag of Soviet productivity would remain valid even if Soviet economic geniuses should discover some revolutionary technologies: the West would adapt them much more rapidly and on a greater scale. Should the Soviet Union keep them secret, they would remain insignificant.

As we have seen, the gross national product of a Communist country is always inferior to that of an equivalent Western country. Does this mean that, because of the insufficient economic yield of a Communist country, the latter must give up all its old aspirations towards domination? Does it mean that the aggressiveness of Communist countries will be diminished? Such a conclusion can definitely *not* be inferred. Professor Kneschaurek, previously quoted, has explained why very clearly. His observations are as valid today as they ever were:

«These assumptions (that is, the slowing down of the Soviet rate of growth which the author has forecast) should naturally not lead us to underestimate the economic development of the Eastern bloc and its dangers; above all because, from a political and military point of view, general economic growth and the development of a country's prosperity are less important than the expansion of «strategic» sectors of the economy. In the Soviet Union and its satellites, it is precisely in these sectors that progress continues at a sustained rhythm, and it is for them that the greatest productive forces and the largest amount of available capital are reserved. The East's real threat lies in the fact that it might surpass in West militarily and politically, not that the whole of its economy might overtake that of the West. Although the total production potential of the Soviet Union and its satellites still represents only a third (or, taken per head of population, only a quarter) of the production potential of the United States and the main Western European states, the volume of production in the militarily important sectors can be estimated as being already today about equal to the Western volume. This relationship clearly shows where the core of the problem is to be found, namely in a significant weight displacement towards Communist countries of the production potential of politically and militarily important sectors.»

These facts have been too often neglected, particularly because the consequences which can be drawn from them appear contradictory. The assertion that the growth of the Communist economy must remain in second place remains as true as the assertion that the aggressive potential of the Communist states is constantly increasing. Here is a very simple example. Of two workers, one, X, earns 2000 francs a month, and Y, only 1000 francs. X leads a life of luxury and spends 1800 francs a month, so that the only saves 200 francs. Y, on the other hand, spends only 600 francs a month, and can therefore put away 400 francs. At the end of the first year, X disposes of a «power» amounting to 2400 francs, while Y in spite of an income which is only half that of X, has a «power» of 4800 francs or exactly the double.

These figures cannot really be applied to the East-West conflict, even though they are not taken altogether at random. The gross national product of the Soviet Union does amount to about half that of the United States, while the living standard of the average Soviet citizen is about a third of the average U. S. standard. Thanks to the enforced limitations of consumer goods, and in spite of growth insufficiency due to the system, the Soviet Union can attribute more economic power to sectors which enable it to expand its power (research, development and production in strategic sectors, propaganda and agitation throughout the world). The fact that the Communist exert so much effort to consolidate a power which pursues aggressive ends, proves not olny the high rate of aggressiveness in Communist regimes, but also their low «degree of humanity»: the population is never asked whether it wishes, or does not wish, this radical reduction in consumer goods.

The consistently aggressive character of Soviet policy can easily be illustrated. In 1965, the Soviet Union had 220 intercontinental ballistic missiles, the U. S. 900; today the Soviets have 1350 I. C. B. Ms, the U. S. 1050. The Soviet missile reserves increase each year by 250 units. The relationship of forces has thus changed.

Some of these considerations are somewhat removed from our topic, the technological gap. But it is important to appreciate the conditions — mainly unfulfilled, as we have seen — in which the Soviet Union would be able to catch up with and overtake Western economies. By the same token, it must be pointed out that the growth of Soviet power has not been jeopardized.

IV. Parallel economies

Quantitative and qualitative comparisons relative to the export and import of high-grade industrial products can be indicative of the levels of technological development in various countries, as well as of other related trends. Machinery is typical of such industrial products.

Comparisons can be based on a number of general considerations. Any developing country must begin by importing all the machinery it needs. During the industrialization process, it will slowly start to produce its own machinery, and will gradually develop a modest export trade aimed mostly at other developing countries. At this stage, the country in question should be importing slightly less machinery; but as industrialization progresses and technology develops, it will be able to export more of its machines, while it will still have to import an increasing amount of more sophisticated machinery. Once its industrial development is fully developed, the country enters the general framework of the international division of labor. The trade volume is broadly determined on the basis of the theory of comparative costs and, taking into account the sizes of the various national economies, tends to show a long-term balance. An example of this kind of development can be seen in Japan, which now both buys and sells machinery to and from the West.

The charts on pages 22 and 23 show Soviet import and export trends in machinery.

The figures are significant, and a number of conclusions can be drawn from them.

In the first place, both Soviet imports and exports increased considerably during the fifties. This was due to the modified autarchic tendencies prevalent in the Soviet Union at the end of the war.

Imports, which developed very rapidly after 1957, were meant to re-establish contact with Western technology. It was what we call the second phase of Soviet industrialization, the first having started in 1928 with the Five Year Plans. It is not surprising that, at the beginning of this new period, the Soviet Union depended upon substantial machinery imports.

During this time, machinery imports moved up from 20 % to 30 %. The Soviet Union leaned heavily on imports from the satellite countries for obvious reasons: prices and delivery dates were set by the Russians themselves. Furthermore, East Germany and Czechoslovakia, the two most industrially advanced satellites, were able to deliver goods of impeccable quality to the Soviet economy.

Machinery imports from the «capitalist» countries increased also. Bearing in mind what was said of a model state at the beginning of this chapter, we would expect a development curve which dips at first, then rises slightly, and, with an increase in exports, continues indefinitely at an horizontal level. And it indeed was how Soviet economic development progressed in the fifties. But it never reached the stabilization stage, the sixties having shown a continuation of the same development without any import increase.

Export figures are particularly interesting. The percentage of machinery exports, within the total export bill, has constantly increased and has even doubled in 20 years, from 10 % to 20 %. But the trend taken by these exports shows that the increase is due only to the greater possibilities provided by the industrialization programs of developed countries. Figures for machinery exports to Western developed countries have remained constant and extremely small, indicating a serious weakness in Soviet technology: in the comparatively long period of twenty years, there has been no basic improvement in the structure of its machinery exports.

The picture becomes even darker when one realizes that the modest increase in machinery exports which did occur can be

Table 1

Imports (in millions of rubles)

	1950	1955	1960	1965	1966	1967	1968
Global imports	1310	2754	5066	7252	7122	7683	8469
of which							
Machinery and equipment (percentage of global exports)	282 (21,5)	833 (30,2)	1508 (29,8)	2423 (33,4)	2308 (32,4)	2625 (34,2)	3127 (36,9)
from							
Socialist states (percentage of machinery imports)	183 (64,8)	660 (79,3)	1088 (72,1)	1964 (81,0)	1803 (78,2)	2021 (77,0)	2316 (74,1)
Capitalist states (percentage of machinery imports)	73 (26,1)	145 (17,4)	406 (26,9)	452 (18,7)	501 (21,8)	597 (22,8)	799 (25,6)
Developing states (percentage of machinery imports)	—	—	—	—	—	—	—
Other states (percentage of machinery imports)	26 (9,1)	27 (3,3)	14 (1,0)	7 (0,3)	5 —	6 (0,2)	12 (0,3)

Table 2

Exports (in millions of rubles)

	1950	1955	1960	1965	1966	1967	1968
Global exports	1615	3084	5007	7357	7957	8687	9571
of which							
Machinery and equipment (percentage of global imports)	191 (11,8)	539 (17,5)	1029 (20,6)	1472 (20,3)	1654 (20,8)	1832 (21,1)	2071 (21,6)
from							
Socialist states (percentage of global imports)	179 (93,7)	514 (95,4)	900 (87,6)	1018 (69,1)	1183 (71,5)	1384 (75,5)	1590 (76,9)
Capitalist states (percentage of machinery imports)	3 (2,0)	10 (1,8)	19 (2,0)	39 (2,8)	60 (3,6)	55 (3,1)	61 (2,9)
Developing states (percentage of machinery imports)	0,1 —	3 (0,5)	105 (10,4)	406 (27,6)	360 (21,8)	y 389 (21,4)	417 (20,2)
Other states (percentage of machinery imports)	8 (4,3)	12 (2,3)	5 —	9 (0,5)	51 (3,1)	3 —	3 —

Source: Vneshniaya Torgovlia SSSR, Moscow 1961, 1967, 1969.

attributed to the fact that satellite countries (which complain about the inferior quality of Soviet products) were forced to accept them, and that, in the framework of economic aid, developing countries received them — and were not exactly satisfied with their experience with Soviet products.

Characteristically, since 1965, the percentage of machinery exports to the developing countries has been steadily diminishing – while exports to the satellites, which the Soviet Union is in a position to bend to its will, have again been increasing.

The disparity in machinery trade between the Soviet Union and the Western states is particularly striking. Soviet imports and exports, as well as export percentages relative to imports, have developed as follows:

Table 3

Trade in machinery with the West

	1950	1955	1960	1965	1966	1967	1968
Imports (in millions of rubles)	73	145	406	452	501	597	799
Exports (in millions of rubles)	3	10	19	39	60	55	61
Exports as percentage of imports	4,1	6,9	4,7	8,6	12,0	9,2	7,6

It can readily be seen that the Soviet Union has not been developing in the manner of a model state in the process of building up its economy and increasing its technological mastery. Soviet dependence on Western technology in particular, and on foreign technology in general, is just as significant if one compares the figures for machinery trade with the West to the overall total of Soviet foreign trade.

Table 4

Percentage of Soviet machinery trade with Western countries as a percentage of overall Soviet foreign trade.

	1950	1955	1960	1965	1966	1967	1968
Imports	5,6	5,3	8,0	6,2	7,0	7,8	9,4
Exports	0,2	0,3	0,4	0,5	0,7	0,6	0,6

Machinery represents about a third of Soviet imports from Western countries, but only 2 % to 3 % of the total exports to these countries. This astonishing disproportion, which barely ever varies, does not appear to be about to change, thus indicating that there is no essential improvement in the Soviet technological level compared to that of the West. A similar disproportion, albeit not as striking, exists between the Soviet Union and Eastern Europe — that is, Eastern Germany and Czechoslovakia primarily. Among Soviet machinery imports, the most important are Western deliveries of machinery for the food, light textile, chemical, wood and cellulose industries, as well as equipment for laboratories, shipbuilding and the production of synthetic goods.

This disparity reveals a typical characteristic of the Soviet economy. The Soviet Union is unable to simultaneously develop its heavy industry (for power) and its light industry (for the production of consumer goods). Political considerations have made it necessary to give priority to the strategic domain. As a result — and to avoid a complete deterioration of light industry — the Soviet Union has bought Western technology. Prototypes are ordered to be copied, thus saving development costs.

Since Stalin's death, the Soviet Union has tried hard to improve its industrial technology by raising the budget for research and development, and by increasing essential imports. In the last fifteen years, the Soviet Union is reported to have spent some 30 billion Swiss francs, paid to the West for machines and equipment, excluding ships. By any comparison, this is a huge sum. About a sixth has been allocated to consumer industries, approximately a third to chemical industries.

Such a spending level should have brought about an economic miracle, if only a modest one. Western Germany, Japan, South Korea and Formosa, for example, have all succeeded in doing just that, but not the Soviet Union. The surge of the fifties, when Soviet technology started to improve in comparison with that of the West, has faded out. Productivity trends indicate that the technological gap has again widened in the sixties.

In an earlier chapter, this deterioration in the productivity rate was attributed to the changing and worsening political climate of that period. This climate affects not only workers, but also the employers: it affects industrial management as such and, finally, also the technology. The question is whether the slowdown in the growth rate can be explained more precisely. Much of the statistical data needed for this purpose is lacking. Nevertheless, several valid considerations can be made.

First, the quality of the labor force. In comparing the fifties with the sixties, and the Soviet Union with the United States, is there any sign of an unfavorable development? The data which we possess do not indicate that there is an essential difference between the fifties and sixties. Apparently, the level of worker training and the amount of women employed has increased more rapidly in the Soviet Union than in the United States. But the Soviet level of worker training has not yet reached the Western level and that is why more women are at work in the Soviet Union than in the West. A reserve manpower force is thus being used in the Soviet Union, a reserve which could be put to better use in the West.

As to the manpower distribution (country versus city), the Soviet Union has had little success in its efforts to draw the work force off the land and into the cities. Industry cannot assimilate quickly enough the many thousands who would like to move to urban centers. Today, as twenty years ago, the percentage of those working on the land is still very high. Here again, there is no essential difference between the fifties and sixties.

Finally, what about wages? Here a definite increase is to be noted everywhere. But again, comparatively little importance can be given to wage growth in the Soviet Union. If we compare the Soviet Union with the West, the former still comes off extremely badly. A lack of economic stimulus is not conducive to productivity growth. From all evidence, the highly significant step from a market of enforced consumption (due to lack of supply) to a free market in consumer goods can never be taken while heavy industry attracts as much priority in economic planning as it has in the Soviet Union during the last twenty years.

From 1950 to 1962, the percentage of Soviet agricultural workers has decreased by the same amount as in Italy: 14 %. In Italy, it has declined from 43 % to 29 %, in the Soviet Union, from 54 % to 40 %. This indicates the Soviet lag in structural change. Considering that, in the future, the reduction rate is likely to decrease rather than increase, the Russians should have tried hard for an accelerated decrease; in order to drop from 40 % to 26 % (Italy's approximate achievement, between 1960 and 1962), the Soviet Union will need more time — unless it is prepared to make a large-scale economic effort to this end.

The reduction of the number of agricultural workers, thanks to a growing agricultural mechanization, allows for a general growth in productivity, resulting in an increase in the overall national product. In the case of Italy, we can attribute part of this increase to the improved and more efficient distribution of the available manpower. In the case of the Soviet Union, if a similar increase in the growth rate is attributed to the distribution of manpower, while also taking into account salary increases and the higher quality of the manpower, the growth rate of Soviet productivity could be determined. Even though it would not be completely void of technological progress, it would show that the economic use made of this progress has been inefficient and that it is likely to be still deteriorating.

Productivity can be affected by many components, all of which can be affecting its rate in different or even opposite ways. Among these, technology and industrial management are the most important. The Soviet lack of efficiency in those two branches goes a long way towards explaining Soviet industrial weakness in the sixties. The Russians seem to have been unable to carry out their investment plans — and this, in turn, has meant that, in the Soviet Union, the return on investment has been less than in the United States and Western Europe over the same period.

If we compare this dark economic picture to the considerable progress made in the strategic field, it is obvious that the Soviet economy is slowly being divided up into two parallel economies, and that every kind of relation between the two seems to be disappearing. The military sector, helped by all economic means available, is growing without any apparent difficulty, while the civilian sector is in constant trouble. The complete separation between the two sectors is astonishing; it allows the military sector to function in nearly complete isolation and to be subsidized at the expense of the civilian sector.

V. Professional training trends

The technological gap between two countries is determined, among many factors, by the training level of manpower: workers, technical staffs and management leaders. However, it is difficult to estimate differences precisely and objectively. Training value does not only depend on its length, but also on the efficiency and intensity with which it is carried out. Another important factor is the economy's need for an influx of college graduates. «The right man in the right place» is a particularly apt motto in the economic context.

Since 1950, Moscow has been striving hard to narrow the gap between the Soviet Union and the West or, more specifically, the United States. Education expenses have risen faster than in the West, at such a rate that the Soviet Union, with a gross national product of about half that of the U. S., has allocated funds amounting to roughly 75 % of the American credits for education. In 1950, it took an average of five years to train a Soviet worker; in 1958, it took seven years and, by 1975, it will require eight years. During the same time-span, the average training period of an American worker has increased form 10,7 to 12,3 years. In the mid-sixties, a comparison listing of workers training-time showed the following figures:

U. S.	11.2 years
Northwestern Europe	9.0 years
U. S. S. R.	6.8 years
Italy	5.3 years

The proportionately faster increase of the Soviet training time should not be overestimated. In fact, because of modern technological requirements, training time should be increased at a slow rate: it is better to reform it than to have it last longer. From an economical point of view, there is no justification for an enforced and accelerated increase in training duration. Each additional training year costs much more than the preceding one. Thus an increase of 10,7 to 12,3 years, as shown by the U. S., is more valuable and more efficient than the Soviet increase of five to seven years effected during the same period.

The Soviet economy has, however, considerably more college graduates at its disposal: the percentage has jumped from 1.7 % in 1950 to 4.6 % in 1968. The corresponding U. S. figures are 6.4 and 11.4 %. Here is a comparative listing of the percentages of college graduates employed in industry during the middle sixties:

U. S.	11.6 %
U. S. S. R.	3.8 %
Northwestern Europe	3.2 %
Italy	2.6 %

Even though the Soviet Union has overtaken Western Europe, this progression has not yet fully shown its effectiveness, due to a certain amount of initial friction problems. But Western Europe is indeed under the threat of being left in the background. In the U. S., the optimum number of college graduates seems to have been reached.

During the period following the Second World War, the Soviet Union — in contrast to the West — has concentrated all its efforts, in the field of college level education, on the departments and institutes of natural and technical sciences, as the Russians had foreseen the growing importance of these two sciences. The program adopted by the Party at the 13th Congress held in 1961 is significant on that point: «The Party will do its utmost to promote the value of science in the organization of Communist society and the prompt and widespread use of scientific data ... Science itself will fully become a productive power.»

At the 23rd Congress of March 1966, Kosygin stated even more specifically that «the development of the economic conflict between the two world systems depends on the rate of growth of our scientific knowledge, and on the extent to which we utilize the result of our research in our production.»

The Soviet Union has thus positively emphasized the training of natural science specialists and, above all, of engineers. The number of engineering degress awarded has become the Soviet symbol of the sixties. The annual number of college graduates has practically doubled since 1955, reaching a global figure of 525,000 in 1968. About half of these are natural or technical science graduates. In the U. S., 675,000 students completed their college studies during the same year: approximately 25 % of them are natural science specialists or engineers.

The Soviet progression seemed to allow the Russian to reach the ambitious goal forecast in the 1961 program, according to which industrial production was to grow by 150 % in order to catch up with that of the U. S., and even attain a sixfold increase to overtake the American industrial output.

The number of engineering degrees awarded was interpreted as the most significant result brought about by this trend in economic policy, and thus was credited with an absolute value. It became a fetish, and it overshadowed other objectives of prime importance such as the training level and the growth in work productivity. Meanwhile, Soviet complaints about deficiencies in the training of engineers and in their work productivity increased considerably.

At the beginning of 1966, Piotr Kapitsa, the well-known atomic scientist, attracted a lot of attention when he bluntly pointed out («Komsomolskaya Pravda», January 20, 1966) that, because of inferior training, the work productivity of Soviet specialists in natural and technical sciences only reached half of of their American colleagues.

Some time later, in 1968, a letter from an engineer named Bakhmatov, from Baku, triggered a flurry of comments. Published in the «Literaturnaya Gazeta», it criticized Soviet scientists in their approach to their work and in their output. Five hundred letters of the same type, sent in by readers, were published in 18 months, thus indicating the importance attached to the position of engineer in present-day Soviet society. In an extensive study, Jan Kotkovski, of the Moscow Institute for the International Worker's Movement, has objectively compared Soviet engineers to their U. S. counter parts.

Unexpectedly, Kotkovski quotes U. S. estimates which indicate that the training level of Soviet engineers is much higher than that of their American colleagues. He then promptly refutes them, arguing that in the Soviet Union 4300 engineers would be needed to reach one billion dollars worth of production, instead of only 1200 in the U. S. The work productivity ratio is thus of 3.6.

An article dated August 5, 1968, by Kulagin, general manager of the Sverdlov Works of Leningrad, points out an interesting phenomenon. The author notices, on the one hand, a decrease in the workers training level: the percentage of workers who attend only five classes appears to be rising (30 % in 1964, 33 % in 1965, 35 % in 1966, and 37 % in 1967). On the other hand, the number of college graduates is growing, which explains why engineers are assigned jobs which could be held by qualified workers. A survey conducted in 240 enterprises has shown that 69 % of the tasks performed by engineers could have been fulfilled by draftsmen, messengers, administrative employees, or secretaries. Obviously, intermediate staffs are lacking in the Soviet Union.

A significant drawback characteristic of Soviet engineers seems to be a more than optimum specialization. In her book «Die Intelligenz im Sowjetreich» (TM 13, I. S. E. Editions, p. 85), Elisabeth Schürer notes that almost every industrial branch «has at its disposal a university, or at least a departement, in which engineers are trained in a very restricted field only. The result of such a specialization is that the graduating students have received an extremely narrow professional training and do not have an overall knowledge of the related branches. It should also be pointed out that those already highly spezialized institutions reveal another even narrower specialization. The institute of peat industry, for instance, includes three departements; there are thus three different kinds of engineers spezialized in peat production: mechanical and technological engineers, machine engineers, and construction engineers.»

Soviet industry, however, is less specialized than its U. S. counterpart as Russian enterprises usually manufacture numerous side products.

For the Soviets, the drawbacks are obvious. The Soviet engineer's high degree of spezialization, on the job and during his training, influences the professional training cost and decreases work possibilities. When the engineer's technical knowledge is not fully utilized, which must frequently happen since Soviet industry is far from being highly specialized, he is forced to divert his activity to another field. Furthermore, two or three highly spezialized engineers must be hired to do a job which a single U. S. engineer could do, thanks to his broad professional training. There are sometimes too many engineers for one job and not enough for another.

The U. S. engineer, whose educational training program is wide-ranging, only specializes when he gets on the job, thus retaining his mobility. The Soviet engineer, on the other hand, is unable to compensate at work for his lack of general professional training.

In a recent book, P. A. Kromov, a Soviet specialist in work productivity has quoted the following index figures for work productivity:

Soviet Union	100
U. S.	300
France	140
West Germany and Great Britain	125—130

To summarize, there are definite deficiencies in Soviet professional training: the scientists are over-specialized while the enterprises are under-spezialized, a situation which results in a waste of engineers. Besides, not enough attention is given to intermediate staffs: the training of the new generation seems to be stagnating.

We have seen that the percentage of college graduates has dropped in the U. S. from 11.6 in 1965 to 11,4 in 1968, while, in the Soviet Union, it has gone up from 3.8 to 4.6. We believe that, considering the present industrialization level in the U. S., the optimum level has been reached. If in the Soviet Union, where loud complaints are already being raised against an excessive number of engineers, an optimum supply of college graduates has also roughly been reached, it means that, by the same token, there is an extremely wide technical gap between the superpowers.

Soviet factory machinery is far from functioning at a maximum level. A survey of machine building plants made in 1964 has revealed that, at the time of the survey, 243,000 machines (19 % of the total number of machines surveyed) were not in operation. «A comparison with similar surveys made in 1962 and 1963 indicate that the index for machinery utilization has evolved on a negative trend» (A. N. Eftimov, «Die Industrie der UdSSR», West-Berlin, 1967, p. 45). «In spite of the high increase rate of production funds (investments), a large part of the equipment supply dates back to 15 or 20 years ago, or more. Such obsolete equipment holds back the increase rate of work productivity and the improvement of production. Furthermore, it is responsible for the unusually high cost of general repairs. The repair cost of all sorts of equipment is often a multiple higher than the value of brand new machinery and equipment. In comparison with the total supply of equipment, the total cost of repairs increases from year to year» (p. 51).

Machinery remains idle because the production schedule cannot be met, or due to a lack of spare-parts. Machinery rusts because, of inferior upkeep and technical care. These are the results of poor work discipline which also affects work productivity. Expenditure increases faster than return, the economic principle is not followed closely enough.

All these items are part of the overall picture of the technological gap between the superpowers.

VI. Research and development

Expenditure for research and development has become an index of a state's industrialization — which essentially includes applied research and product development up to prototype level. The research and development expenditure of a country, of an industrial branch, or of an enterprise, is closely related to competitive ability and to planned endeavor, as long as this expenditure is economically sound.

How can profitability of research and development expenditure be measured?

In countries with a market economy, this question is of minor importance; competition which always exists, at least potentially, forces each manufacturer (even the State when acting as a manufacturer) to take special account of the profitability of research and development expenses. Improfitable investment not only diminishes possible gains, but also jeopardizes the very existence of an enterprise.

To the objection that total competition is no longer guaranteed, it can be retorted that the relative and always potential competition existing in any democracy is sufficient.

Moreover, Western economy's growing concentration has been considered as a threat to the market system, for it sometimes displays characteristics not unlike those of the Communist planned economy.

This pessimistic point of view seems totally unrealistic. It overlooks the fact that the concentration trend in economics is a necessary phenomenon, if national borders are gradually to be abolished. In the wider areas of the European Economic Community or the European Free Trade Association, there is a need for larger enterprises ,although the latter should not exert too strong an influence or develop monopolist tendencies. Competition exists even in these broader areas. This encompasses economic organizations and all larger enterprises.

Such is not the case in a planned and centrally directed economic system. Responsibility for business decisions is not divided among many responsible individuals, but concentrated in a bureaucratic and supreme organization. Erroneous decisions are more damaging and can only be slowly corrected. Most of all, institutional economic coercion cancels mobility and adaptability to changing conditions. Worse yet, the state organization exerts an institutional and political restraint preventing mobility and adaptibility, because, in contrast to democratic business conditions, consequences are more influential than competences. In the Communist planned economy — as opposed to a market economy — the industrial leader will be much more reluctant to experiment with new combinations of production factors and to open new markets through research and development. Possible errors of judgement are sanctioned far too severely and successful ventures are hardly rewarded in spite of the premium system.

The anonymous bureaucracy is responsible for all important decisions. Most subjective errors are thus avoided and personal responsibilities are limited. But objective errors are that much more important. Adaptability, institution, and imagination, these vital proponents of progress, can no longer flourish.

The limited value of comparative research and development figures between East and West should again be pointed out, since they are not calculated according to the same standards.

Surveys made by the OEEC have revealed that in 1967 the Soviet Union spent 23,7 billions of dollars for research and development, the U. S. 23,8 billions. In 1968, these expenditures reached respectively 25.8 and 25 billion dollars: for the first time, the Soviet figures were higher than the U. S. ones — an important achievement for the Soviet Union which had already surpassed Western Europe.

During the last few years, Europe has been living above its means: it has been consuming too much and not reinvesting enough. Nevertheless, Soviet efforts and output are highly significant. In spite of a much smaller gross national product, the Soviet Union has been able to contribute as much to research and development as the U. S.

Does that mean that the Soviet Union is now able to close the technological gap separating it from the U. S., or possibly to take the lead? This is unlikely, even if the Russians could spend more — and at a faster rate — for research and development than the U. S. The reasons for this are manifold and are inherent in the Soviet political system.

- The Soviet political system cannot provide enough material and moral incentives to increase work productivity decisively.
- The Soviet political system is unable to enforce on a working basis a large-scale economic plan, since the human being is not an electronic brain. And yet, for political reasons, it cannot afford to relinquish its competence to a small-scale economic plan.
- The Soviet political system must set up two different economic systems; one being power oriented and highly developed, the other consumer-oriented and underdeveloped. Both systems must be kept apart from each other — implying a certain amount of inefficiency.

One could assume, at first glance, that Soviet salaries for research and development employees would be lower than in Western Europe or in the United States especially. This is, however, not necessarily so since highly-qualified specialists draw amazingly high salaries in Communist countries. They are often paid twenty to fifty times more than the average worker (as compared to two to ten times more in the West). Their salaries will probably soon reach the absolute Western level.

If research and development expenditure is undoubtedly higher in the Soviet Union than in the West, the infrastructure is weaker. When research contracts are assigned, problems due to an overly rigid planning system must be solved, or brand new research centers have to be built from the ground up. Here again, Soviet economic adaptibility is far less flexible thant that of the Western market economy.

Furthermore, in the Communist system of a planned economy, expenses for research and development are usually earmarked for heavy industry to the detriment of other economic sectors. In comparison with the West, a substantial improvement of the entire economic situation would require — relatively as well as absolutely — much higher research and development expenditures.

Finally, Soviet expenditure for research and development is not judiciously distributed. Much more — too much apparently — is spent on research than on development: about twice the U. S. amount spent on basic research (U. S.: 9 %　of the research and development expenses, U. S. S. R.: 20 %), while U. S. expenditure for development amounts to two-thirds of the total amount spent on research and development. In the Soviet Union, the ratio between the theorists (research) and the experts (development) is of approximately one to one, while the ideal ratio should be one to twenty. So much time elapses between applied research and mass production that the final product is often obsolete when it eventually appears on the market.

The Soviet attempt to develop their own small car, the Zaporozhets, illustrates this phenomenon. Six years went by and substantial funds were spent before Russian engineers realized that their prototype could not possibly be competitive with current Italian or West German automobiles. The whole project was abandoned and Fiat was asked to set up a plant in the Soviet Union for the production of its own 124 model.

The Soviet conception of research and development, as well as the training of Russian engineers, is much too systematic.

On October 23, 1968, a new regulation was published on «measures taken to improve the efficiency of scientific organizations and to increase the use of scientific and technical knowledge in economy.» Shortly thereafter, »Komsomolskaya Pravda» of December 26, 1968, announced that «today, Communism is waging an important fight against capitalism; production is its battlefield, science and technology are its weapons.»

In 1961 already, a State Committee for the coordination of scientific research was formed. This organization is mainly in charge of coordination, but it shares the corresponding competences with the State planning board and the Academy of

Sciences. The advice of the Ministry of Finance carries a lot of weight and control by the Party is guaranteed by the department of «Sciences and higher Academies» of the Central Committee of the Soviet Communist Party.

Such an organization implies that no effort has been spared and, since all endeavors in the research and development field receive political priority, ever-increasing means are undoubtedly available. The Soviet Union can afford the cost, particularly considering that, compared to democratic states, it tends to disregard the Soviet people's demand for consumer goods.

However, it is unlikely that, by a mere increase in research and development expenditure — and without modification of its political system, the Soviet Union can raise its economy to a higher level than that of democratic countries.

Sakharov, the Russian scientist, compares the United States and the Soviet Union to two skiers: the U. S. skier is ahead, leaving a trail which makes it easier for the Soviet skier to follow him and to catch up with him. Yet the second skier lacks the necessary spurt of energy to overtake the first.

The Soviet Union, because of its governmental regimentation, simply does not have the means required to overtake the U. S.:
– from an economic standpoint, it lacks a market in which production can be economically successful;
– from a political standpoint, it lacks the conditions in which work productivity can increase.

The Russians themselves are well aware of this situation. They have initiated reforms in an attempt to introduce elements of market economy into their planned economy and achieve a more efficient distribution of production factors. In this sense, market and economic conditions are closely related. When the elements of market economy become strong enough to bring about an improvement of economic conditions, they boost the consumer's economy at the expense of the power-oriented economy, and thus jeopardize Communist efforts to reach their goal.

This does not imply that there is never going to be any progress: rising expenditures for research and development will certainly lead to improvements. But the economic output of Communist-led countries cannot in any way be compared to that of democratic countries. The technological gap and the economic downward trend will remain constant, even if the output of the power-oriented sector of the economy should bring it to first place.

In order to try to win the race with the West, the Soviet Union must pay the price: a chronically lagging consumer's economy. Strict control and supervision of the population must be enforced through political totalitarianism.

As long as the Communist movement pursues an aggressive policy and strives for a position of supremacy, it will have to remain totalitarian. Should it decide to do without totalitarianism, it will also have to give up its aggressive goals. The technological gap could then lessen and the consumer's economy, as well as the economy in general, could improve its output. But then the movement and the political system would no longer be Communist — in today's sense of the word.

VII. Market economy and planned economy

We have repeatedly pointed out that the Soviet Union's economic output will always be second rate and that the economic system is essentially responsible for this. At this point, the differences between a market economy and a planned economy should be more closely examined, particularly since it has become fashionable both to praise the planned economy system, in spite of its failures, and to attack the market economy concept in spite of its higher performances.

In Western Germany, left-wing students demand that universities should teach only socialist — read Communist — economics, while in Cuba, Fidel Castro has to admit publicly the failure of his socialist economic experiments. Confusion of the minds is a surprising phenomenon to be added to the recent and important problems of our time.

The ways and means by which modern technology can be propagated through economic structures are the object of our study in this chapter.

In a market economy, new technology expands rapidly and in a nearly biological manner. Its main champions are found in private enterprise — which exists by competition and the need to make a profit, two factors which are usually considered as the main propelling forces working toward a dynamic and progressive approach in economics. But profit and competition make certain demands of their own. These include a continual search for new cost-saving devices and their prompt adaptation to all branches of the economy, thus ensuring a fast propagation of economic improvements.

Profit and competition also stimulate the introduction of new products as well as the development of copies and of competitive products.

This almost invisible process results inevitably in the abandonment of obsolete technology and the disappearance from the market of outdated products.

The task of governments — even when they themselves do not provide the economic motive forces — should be to stimulate and also to partly finance such developments, by the use of appropriate fiscal policies for example. Competition between producers — each of whom is looking for profit — even leads to technological improvements in military techniques, although governments are the only customers for military hardware. Since, in a market economy, the military sector cannot be kept isolated from the civilian sector, military and space technology have civilian ramifications which are bound to surface sooner or later.

Finally, most international companies founded since the Second World War promote the development of modern technology and of new methods of industrial management by investing in their foreign branches. This propagation process of new technology is, of course, not without obstacles. A few of these are monopolies, patents and industrial secrecy, as well as the difficulty of raising the necessary capital, which may mean that a development of consumer value does not materialize.

Incidentally, it is politically relevant to point out here that Marxism-Leninism has always had as one of its principle tenets «the struggle against monopolies», or against «monopoly-capitalism». One of Lenin's arguments was that monopolies tend towards a profit inflation which deprives the worker of his just reward.

Ironically, the situation of the worker is infinitely better under «monopoly-capitalism» than under the planned economy. Furthermore, with the accelerated technical progress and in the prevailing competitive climate, monopolies no longer represent the threat which they once implied. Profits made by monopolies, such as they have been pictured by Marxism, have been used for the formation of new capital, an indispensable condition for fundamental technical innovation and for the rapid rise in the living standard which derives from it.

Without profit, there can be no economic development. This seems a good enough reason to dispel any prejudice there may be against this economic principle. A practical example can best explain why.

The chemical industry benefits from high profits, a fact which can be considered as particularly shocking since the remedies which it develops are intended to cure illness and it is seen as unjust that profit should be made from helping the sick. This is why in India it has been suggested that the patent protection for pharmaceutical products should be limited to five years. Pharmaceutical monopolies would thus be eliminated, competition would be higher and prices lower. While obvious at first, this concept is, however, much too superficial.

The development of new drugs is extremely expensive. It requires such large funds that only companies of worldwide importance can afford to promote it on a large scale. This high cost is reflected in the price of drugs which is much higher than the simple costs of material and production might imply. Any one drug must remain on the market a long time before the development cost is recuperated — and it is only then that its price can be brought down. The profits thus obtained are then used for the development of new drugs.

A reduction of patent protection to five years would certainly result in a price drop of those medicaments at present on the market. But chemical companies would then begin to lack capital for research and development — all because five years after the appearance of a new product it could be copied and put on the market at a cut-price. Imitators would make the profits, and inventors would carry the losses. Nevertheless, the price of pharmaceutical products could have been lowered; but then new drugs would not have been developed, or the State would have had to subsidize the chemical and pharmaceutical industries. And the State in turn would have to raise taxes to increase its own financial resources. Thus, a reduction in the price of pharmaceutical products would have to be compensated by a tax increase.

Thus, monopolistic tendencies, patents, and trade secrets can contribute to the formation of capital and, in this function, are fully justified, economically speaking. Although they tend to temporarily delay the propagation of technical innovations, they promote the development of new technologies.

In the centralized Soviet economy, there is no automatic mechanism promoting technological development. The elimination of profit and competitive incentives brought the economy to the edge of collapse in 1920, at which time there was an attempt to stimulate profit and competition in the form of «premiums» and of «socialist emulation» respectively. These remained mainly ineffective and would remain so as long as they were kept out of market economics. But market economics were always ruled out for being detrimental to heavy industry, the State's fundamental basis for its aggressive international policies. It thus became the role of the bureaucracy to introduce new technology and new products by means of regulation and decrees. Outdated technology and obsolete products were withdrawn in the same manner.

This is a complicated process which can only be briefly outlined here. In the framework of long-term planning (about twenty years) and of medium-term planning (about five years), concrete yearly plans are drawn up. Each plant or factory is asked to list its production requirements (in terms of workers, area, and capital) and to submit them to higher authority. These data are then assembled by sectors of industry and integrated by the State Planning Commission into a single plan-project submitted to the State and Party authorities. At that stage, important modifications are usually made for political reasons, and the National Economic Plan is enacted into a law. From the top on down to lower levels (the initial procedure being reversed) — the new law finally reaches the factory in the form of a series of practical and compulsory regulations.

This process would be complicated enough if it were just a matter of increasing the production rates of existing technologies and products. But when it becomes a question of introducing new technologies and new products, the Plan seizes up.

Soviet industrial innovations are usually worked out by research and planning departments which are controlled by ministries and other organs of government. Advisory reports are coordinated at the top by the State Committee for Science and Technology and by the State Planning Commission (Gosplan), and then again, farther down the scale, by numerous industrial ministries.

An order given to an enterprise to manufacture a new product starts a chain reaction which has to be taken into consideration by the planning authorities: an increase of the labor force may be necessary, or the qualifications required may have to be modified. New machinery, new equipment, or even new factories may be needed. Production plans of other enterprises (suppliers, distributors) have to be adapted.

In brief, the development and distribution of new products in the Soviet Union is an administrative operation which has to be effected in a centralized manner by a bureaucracy which is naturally very heavy-handed. This explains why innovations in Soviet economy are fewer and require more time to be enforced than in the West. This is especially true of the consumer industry, but not of heavy industry.

The increase in economic bureaucracy, although inevitable, is one of the main reasons for the lack of mobility and the general backwardness in the Soviet planned economy. However, there is another reason — perhaps an even more important one — in the fact that the system of economic stimulation is completely counter-productive: the lower level (individual enterprises) and middle level (ministries) organisations are wholly opposed to innovation and do not generally stray from beaten paths.

In spite of all reforms, the success of an enterprise is always judged according to how it fills its share of the Plan. If it fails to fill its quota, it loses its premiums; but if production exceeds the prescribed norm, the enterprise receives additional premiums as well as rewards for the administrative personnel. Other economic criteria, such as the extent to which new technology is introduced, generally play a secondary role.

Innovation always contains an element of risk. Production may be stopped because of a lack of workers or machinery, while many forms of teething troubles may arise, such as late delivery of essential parts from other factories. This is the sort of thing which threatens plan fulfilment. Administrators and heads of enterprises consequently adopt a hesitant attitude to industrial innovation — particularly since managers often find that if they are successful their plan quotas are modified upwards as a result. Innovations are thus not welcome; managers are not only opposed to them, but also often disobey or ignore orders to carry them through. They usually put the blame on inadequate and delayed deliveries of material and equipment. Often enough, they are protected by the ministries themselves, since these also are judged by the degree in which their dependents fulfill the relevant portions of the Plan.

The Soviet Government has certainly been aware for a long time that the institutional side of this problem serves as a brake to stimulating technical progress. There has been an attempt to circumvent the difficulty by issuing decrees which are supposed to hasten the introduction of new technology. But decrees of this kind are too often taken merely as managerial exhortations and wishful thinking. The policy of issuing premiums for innovations has had little more success because these are rarely planned in an objective manner and therefore very rarely have any durable stimulus. The history of Soviet economic reforms over the last ten years is largely one of trying to achieve increased technological innovation by a series of extremely clumsy methods. Their effect has been very limited.

Other drawbacks of the system have already been pointed out, namely that heavy industry (the military sector) and consumer industry (the civilian sector) have been completely isolated from each other, and that innovations are usually worked out in research departments which have little contact with industrial enterprises. The economic planning system as a whole has also been the cause for the lack of reserves, either of raw materials or manufactured goods.

The lack of valid production incentives, the bottlenecks in the planned economy, the gap between heavy industry and consumer goods industry, the poor work-productivity record, all these are contributing factors to the economic deficiencies which are so assiduously reported by the Soviet press, but which are, nevertheless, far from easy to eliminate.

It takes, for example, five to seven years to build a factory in the Soviet Union instead of one to three years in the West. A member of the Soviet Academy of Sciences, Trapeznikov, who is also Deputy Chairman of the State Committee for Science and Technology, published an article in «Pravda» on July 7, 1969, dealing with the problems of time-wasting and time-saving. With considerable perception, he noted that in Japan it took nine months to build a new motorcycle factory and that, also in Japan, only two years elapsed between the initial planning stage of a synthetic rubber plant and the actual start of production. «In capitalist countries», writes Trapeznikov, «speed in the execution of orders is the most important form of competition. Delivery dates are generally respected to the day and hour. An inefficient enterprise pays fines for delays, loses customers, and eventually becomes bankrupt. Consequently, rapid application of scientific innovation is given high priority.»

Trapeznikow continues by saying that in the Soviet Union profitability is generally very low. Capital lies unused, transport is too slow, and so much time elapses between planning and mass production that any innovation is obsolete before it appears on the market.

Technical progress is also greatly hampered by the lack of market prices. Soviet prices are fixed by centralized edict, based on average industrial costs — and thus completely rigid. They give no reliable indication of substitution possibilities in economic terms. Writing-off outdated equipment in economic calculation is considered as a capitalist custom. Capital is supplied according to arbitrary considerations.

On average, industrial equipment in the Soviet Union is made to last between fifteen and twenty years as against about ten years in the United States. It is by no means rare throughout Soviet industry — particularly in textiles — to find equipment over fifty years old. Five hundred thousand of the lathes are more than twenty years old and still in use.

Rapid equipment renewal is both a cause and a consequence of rapid technological development. The backwardness of Soviet economy in modernizing its plants and industrial equipment is added proof of the technological gap which separates it from the West.

The use of obsolete industrial equipment — there are, for example, two hundred foundries in the Soviet Union which are not yet mechanized — is an element which significantly diminishes profitability. It thus influences the overall economic output (which always remains in second place) and entails financial contributions at the Soviet people's expense.

VIII. Reforms in store?

What about the positive effects which may have resulted from the economic reform? Rather than a historical rundown of the reform itself, the following will be an attempt to evaluate the effects of the measures taken and to ascertain whether the economic reforms will enable the Soviets to make up their lag.

Khrushchev stands in history an a promoter of economic reform. Since his disappearance from politics, Moscow not only still talks of reforms but has indeed introduced several of them. The current Party and State leaders could not ignore their urgency.

Massive financial subsidies which had been the traditional Soviet remedy for economic difficulties could obviously no longer be used since they had consistently remained ineffective. During the sixties, the Soviet expenditure for science trebled while the amount of personnel in research and development organizations doubled. Gold reserves were nearly exhausted due to the purchase of Western factories and equipment which served as virtual «injections» of technology. Yearly investments increased much faster than the gross national product. And yet, returns of new investments decreased regularly while in the West new investment returns are kept at a high level — or even increase.

Actually, even though Soviet experts realized that the technological growth rate had to be increased, they still did not succeed in improving the economic output. Reports dating from the sixties and dealing with the difficulties encountered in the development and introduction of the new technology contrast significantly with the glowing forecast made during the second half of the fifties. Renewed debates on reforms which the Soviets hoped would cure their economic troubles were to follow.

As it has already been pointed out, possibilities for changes within the Soviet system were extremely limited. In order to be fully effective, reforms should introduce economic and ideologic incentives which would lead to a substantial increase of work productivity. A reform program should include:
- a decentralization of economic responsibility at the employer's level, which implies:

- a truly competitive system leading to the elimination of marginal enterprises;
- an increase in the production of consumer goods or, in other words, the promotion of a market economy at the expense of heavy industry and a limitation of the worker's exploitation by the State;
- the acknowledgement of consumer's sovereignty: consumer's demand should be able to determine production.

This type of reform program would undoubtedly prove to be economically successful. But it would require a political price which a Communist regime cannot pay without self-denial: it would loose its grip on the people as well as the basis for its policy of aggression. This is why Communist economic reforms are totally unable to deal straightforwardly with the problems at hand. They can merely try to increase economic efficiency and rationality within a limited field of action.

During the last five years, postulates as well as accomplishments were of two different kinds: the first regulating the centralization of economic planning and administration, the second dealing with the structural principles according to branch, area, or function. With the elimination of the regional economic boards, introduced by Khrushchev in 1957, and with the setting-up of 18 ministries of industry, the extensive economic reforms of September 1965 had emphasized the branch principle instead of the regional one. In 1963, with the creation of the Supreme Economic Board of the Soviet Union, economic planning became even more centralized and has basically remained the same since then. A new economic system was inaugurated. Enterprises could operate with more economic freedom which was expected to enable production to serve as a profit incentive in an attempt to maintain the unity and the trend of the new technological policy.

According to official publications, Soviet reform attempts can be divided in three different groups:
- improvement of the planning and production incentive system;
- introduction of more realistic price fixing;
- reorganization of research and development.

In 1965, the reform of the planning and production incentive system was initiated in most enterprises as the new economic system. According to the latter, the competence of works managers in the elaboration of the Plan is broadened; gain and capital yield are to be used as yardsticks of achievement and as basis for subsidies; capital interests will be taken into account as cost factors. Works managers could thus adjust to demand more efficiently and, most of all, could utilize new technologies and eliminate obsolete equipment in order to lower costs. The enterprise itself was expected to benefit from this cost reduction.

Most enterprises experimented with the new economic system over a period of many years, at least in some instances. There was, however, very little improvement in the economic situation and, for several reasons, no hope for positive results in the future.

On the one hand, due to the aggressive policy of the State, heavy industry still gets top priority as too large a percentage of the overall economic production is withdrawn from internal consumption. Consequently, the conditions of a seller's market will prevail and prevent the development of a real — thus profitable — market production. According to Hans-Herman Höhman («Wirtschaftsreformen in Csteuropa», Cologne 1968), «the obstacles to a reform are linked to the fact that a decentralized planning system, in which enterprises benefit from a growing freedom of decision and commercial initiative, call for more highly qualified works managers than a centralized planning system.» Genuine enterprise managers simply do not exist in the Soviet Union.

On the other hand, the training of enough managers in a relatively short time meets the strong and jealous opposition of the works managers and officials of the planning authorities, as well as the resistance of the Party which is obviously opposed to the creation of a new social class liable to threaten its autonomy and its power. The new managerial class would only be economically effective if it could adapt production to the market. But this would be against Plan regulations since it would be incompatible with the power policy of the Soviet regime. For this very reason and in spite of all reform intentions, the main sources of economic difficulties were retained. Central organizations still determine production input and output, investments, technological improvements, raw materials, semi-finished products, factory installations, even manpower. They also set the standards by which the success of an enterprise should be measured.

Finally, the economic system must be observed to the letter. Technological improvements, or an increase in work productivity, are closely followed by an increase in the production quota, a phenomenon which can hardly be expected to promote work or economic development in the civilian sector.

Even though the reform of the planning and incentive system appears to be headed in the right direction, it has not been able to make much headway. It has resulted in a «mixed, functionally weak system» (Tuchtfeldt) more inclined to avoid all reforms than to ensure their successful application. As previously, bonus increases will be closely related to the fulfilment of the Plan's requirements. A works manager must therefore be very cautious when it comes to introducing new technologies because of the added risks involved. Soviet prices being «unrealistic», the interest-on-capital factor will prevent a machinery renewal while the amortization of the mechanical equipment will be more difficult to estimate than previously. An attempt to bring production more directly in line with the consumer's demand resulted in increased production costs. Several textile factories, which were among the first enterprises to apply the new economic system, soon became unprofitable made-to-order firms. Many complicated and disconcerting managerial policies were retained, such as the award of special bonuses for the introduction of new technologies, the manufacture of new products, or the improvement of older ones. However, under the new system, such overhead costs are the responsibility of the company itself.

Stronger disciplinary regulations are supposed to contribute to the increase of work productivity. On the other hand, the «Shtshekino experiment» is being tested out in 26 enterprises. Their managers can dismiss personnel and distribute the salaries thus saved as bonuses among the other employees. If this procedure should be generalized, it would be the first indication of Soviet unemployment.

Caught in the maelstrom of managerial directives aimed indiscriminately at him by the bureaucracy, the works manager finds it more difficult to make his own decisions *after* than *before* the reform. The reform turns out antiproductive.

So far as prices are concerned, the Soviet Union and its direct sphere of influence in Eastern Europe represent an isolated phenomenon. Prices are determined by an arbitrary system. Although not without limits — facts cannot be ignored — it has nevertheless been stretched quite far.

A centralized price fixing has been the most important tool used for the economic structural change. Prices were set without cost consideration or consumer's demand. They could be arbitrarily lowered through subsidies, or raised through taxes at the political leaders' whim. Since they lacked the reality of cost or demand, they failed to inform the works manager on the type and quantity of products he should be manufacturing, or on their purpose and suggested production time. This type of information was available only in the form of administrative regulations, often arbitrarily determined.

Within the frame of the 1965 economic reform, a price committee was added to the planning board. Its task was to introduce a reform of the price fixing system. Higher prices were fixed with due consideration to capital interest, thus avowing that the latter, often scorned for not being a result of work, cannot be ignored if a production is to reach a maximum economic output. Furthermore, the fact that Socialist economy has often looked for guidance from the world price market is significant: it shows that arbitrary price fixing can be a dangerous falsification.

In spite of the new price fixing system, attempts to influence works managers are still being made, although perhaps in a more up-to-date manner: the price committee was expressly requested to strengthen the role of prices in order to promote technological progress on all levels. The bureaucracy, which was reinforced for that very purpose, tries to determine prices to the last detail and thus to encourage works managers into replacing their old machinery with new equipment. But the price relations chosen can all too easily lead to an exaggerated — and economically unsound — equipment renewal. Therefore, prices for each product must be highly flexible, due to rapidly changing conditions. To achieve this successfully, planners at the top should have an extensive and minute overall knowledge of the economic situation, which is practically impossible even for such an over-developed bureaucracy.

To fix market prices when there is no market is an endeavor which defies description, but an army of Soviet bureaucrats appears determined to make it materialize. The inevitable result will be that the decision-making process will become more involved and that the economy will be plagued with an overdose of bureaucracy until the regime resorts again to increased centralization since, for political reasons, decentralization — albeit economically essential — cannot be tolerated.

In October 1968, new regulations for a restructuration of the organization and the increase of incentive in the field of research and development were officially promulgated. According to the decree, the State Committee for Science and Technology was to coordonate the application of these regulations which were actually put into effect in early 1969. Since they have only been in use for a relatively short time, an objective appreciation of their efficiency cannot yet be made.

The decree basically applies the reform principles of 1965 to the field of research and development. Scientist's salaries and bonuses, as well as the output of research centers, must be based on the economic efficiency of their performance. Organizational measures must allow costs to drop and the ties with production to be strengthened.

But, once again, bureaucratic stodginess and fear of innovation, mixed with envy of innovators, will probably be obstacles which will not be easily evercome. Restructurations determined by the new regulations will cause delays, confusion, and dissatisfaction. Nevertheless, academies and universities will be periodically checked for efficiency, according to the procedure used in industry, so that work produced in institutions of learning should be more in line with industrial requirements and utilized more intensively in applied research.

Unforeseen difficulties could arise. Since they aim for huge and mostly power-oriented collective achievements, dictatorships have always given privileged treatment to scientists, engineers, and artists. As these professions are void of scientific criteria for success and of political responsibility, their members thus benefit from more freedom of action and from a standard of life higher then average. Such professions have become intellectually and materially so attractive that they have been able to ward of internal emigration. The new regulations are likely to restrict considerably the advantages — both intellectual and material — offered by these professions and a replacement problem might have to be solved.

Unable to get to the core of the trouble ailing Soviet economy, the economic reform has failed to provide a remedy. It has only managed to bring about an improvement in rationality and efficiency within narrow and politically motivated boundaries. Following the Western example, the Soviet Union has adopted concepts and criteria used in a market economy such as prices, sales, profits, interests, without being able to develop a market economy. Instead, the Soviets used the same methods as before to manage their economy: ever-increasing — and thus more cumbersome and more bureaucratic — planification and administration.

Consequently, it is doubtful that scientific and technological progress in the Soviet Union can be accelerated. Today more than ever, technological development is a highly dynamic process which requires true initiative and a growing mobility. In the Soviet Union, however, the State is the only employer and its subordinates are bureaucrats opposed to changes and notoriously narrow-minded. Furthermore, the Soviet educational policy enforces the narrow spezialization of scientists and engineers who, upon graduation, are hardly apt at being employers.

The only nations likely to take the lead in the technological race are those which possess economic and scientific institutions capable of prompt action and immediate adaptation. Due to the ever-increasing pace of modern development, the technological gap between the superpowers is bound to widen to the prejudice of the Soviet Union. This could even eventually apply to heavy industry, the production of the most advanced weapons, and space-travel.

Appendix

The technological gap as seen in a comparison of Soviet and U. S. industrial branches

1. Introduction

In the last few years, it has become evident that the elan shown by Soviet industry in the middle fifties has vanished. Spectacular achievements, such as the first Sputnik and the first man in space, have remained without a sequel. Khrushchev's optimistic 1960 prophecy that Soviet technology would catch up with that of the U. S. by 1970, and overtake it by 1980, has given way to a more cautious, even pessimistic outlook. Although the technological gap between East an West had begun to decrease in the fifties, it started increasing again in the sixties. All signs indicate that this development can hardly be halted unless there should be reforms similar to those which were abruptly halted at Prague in the spring of 1968.

It is therefore important to compare the present technology levels in the most highly industrialized sectors of the Soviet Union, the United States, and, as much as possible, Western Europe. A comparison of this kind is necessarily fragmentary and generalized. Its sole aim is to provide an overall survey in practical terms.

Even though there are many other important factors to be considered, this survey will be mostly limited to technological aspects. Quantitative and qualitative limitations in the Soviet economic performance are not exclusively due to technological backwardness. Moscow's central economic administration is inefficient and bogged down in routine; the prevailing social and political climates prevent any decisive growth in work productivity; economic priorities are given for reasons which have nothing to do with economics; because of the lack of a free market, there is no regulative power of prices.

The following sector comparison is a compilation of numerous opinions and impressions gathered from extensive reading and many conversations. It is an attempt to encompass an objective general view of present-day conditions.

2. Industry in general

The average technological level in Soviet industrial production, as compared with the level in the Soviet economy overall, can be assumed to be higher than in a similar comparison in the West. In other words, the technological gap between the Soviet Union and the West is smaller in industry as a whole than in the consumer and distributive industries, because of the priority given to the requirements of heavy industry.

Consequently, there are enormous differences in the technological levels of the different industrial sectors — far greater than in the West. Similarly, there are wider differences of technological level between individual Soviet factories belonging to the same sector: installations operating with completely obsolete machinery can be found next to model enterprises. Marginal enterprises are phased out with great difficulty because of the lack of a competitive climate provided by genuine market conditions. Model factories dispose of a technology which is as high as the average technological level in the West, and sometimes even higher.

Roughly speaking, Soviet technology probably comes nearest to that of the West in machinery, electronics and metallurgy, particularly insofar as these have political and military relevance. Coal-mining and industries based on timber, textile and food industries are especially backward, while chemicals, petroleum, electricity, and construction appear to be at an intermediate stage.

3. Electric power

The Soviet Union boasts the second greatest electric power industry in the world (1969: 689 kWh). Nevertheless, installed capacity and annual production are less than half those of the United States: 2686 kWh per head of population in Russia compared to 7436 kWh in the U.S. This difference reflects mostly the much higher American use of electrical energy for non-industrial uses.

The biggest power stations in the world, both hydraulic and thermal, have been built in the Soviet Union. Still, so far as size of units and advanced technology are concerned, the Soviet Union remains some five years behind the United States in the conventional thermal power engineering. The Soviet lag is even greater in the fields of automation and computer control systems for production and distribution of energy. In the largest Soviet conventional and nuclear power stations, control and data logging systems now in use are generally comparable to those first used in the United States about ten years ago. There are still no Soviet power stations under direct automatic control from a computer system whereas in the United States a number of them have been built since 1963.

Thermal generating equipment with a capacity of 500 mega-watts (MW) has been operating in the U. S., and a number of units with a capacity of up to 1000 MW are in use. The latter operate at supercritical parameters of temperature and steam pressure (respectively 750 degrees Fahrenheit and 3200 pounds) by which water is turned into dry steam without boiling. In the Soviet Union on the other hand, units with a capacity of only 300 MW formed the mainstay of the project for thermal power plants until the end of 1970.

The first 500 MW generator has recently been built near Nosarovsk and the first to reach 800 MW is under construction in Slovyansk. Plans are also underway for 1200 MW generating equipment, but several years will be required before it becomes operative.

It is only now — seven years after the Soviet thermal stations first started producing power — that full production capacity is being slowly reached. These plants had previously not been able to operate on a permanent basis at design level and the expected fuel saving did not materialize. This unsatisfactory performance is mainly due to failures in boiler units which often break down because of metallurgical defects in boiler drums and tubes. The high rate of turbine failures originates from casting defects, inefficient handling of molten metal, and poor welding, as well as from faulty valves, pumps, and couplings. Experiments are being made with 500 to 800 MW steam units, although the 300 MW units used until now have yet to reach production at design level.

The Soviet Union has kept pace with the latest technological development in the production of electricity by nuclear energy. Research has been extensive and experiments have been made with all the various reactor concepts of interest in the West. The number of nuclear power plants, both for research purposes and for commercial use, has been limited in the hope that technological progress will bring about a lowering of capital and operating costs which will make nuclear energy fully competitive with conventional thermal energy.

In the United States, on the other hand, the competitiveness of private industry has led to the construction of a larger number of demonstration and commercial-size nuclear power stations, even though they were not yet economically competitive.

At the end of 1968, the Soviet Union disposed of a capacity of more than 1200 MW in nuclear power plants, of which at least 600 Megavolt-amperes (MVA) were provided by the dual-purpose Siberian power plant. At the same time, Great Britain had a nuclear capacity of 4200 MW and the United States one of 2700 MW. Between 1968 and 1975, the United States are expected to more than double their number of nuclear power plants bringing the total number from 42 to 88, while in the Soviet Union the increase is expected to be from 6 to 13, Russia thus remaining in fifth place on the world scale.

The planning and construction costs of the most recent Soviet nuclear power plants have been considerably lowered. Their operating costs compare favorably with those of the most advanced American nuclear power stations in operation at present. All Soviet nuclear power plants are now built according to a standard plan which provides for two blocks of MWe (megawatts electric); each block contains one pressurized water reactor and two MWe turbogenerators. The reactors in the newest American nuclear power plants dispose of a single turbogenerator with a capacity of 800 to 1300 MWe.

The Soviet Union has overtaken the United States in the construction of more advanced fast breeder reactors which produce more fissionable material than they consume — a significant achievement. The U. S. built the first breeder reactor, the small EBR-1, which came into operation in 1951; between 1963 and

1966, the Americans were using what is thus far the biggest breeder in the world, the Enrico Fermi of Edison Detroit, which had a nuclear operating capacity of 200 MWt (Megawatts thermal). The only U. S. breeder reactor in operation today is the EBR-2, designed to reach 17,4 MWe or 62,5 MWt, but which is far from having reached this capacity. It became operative in 1962 and has about the same designed capacity as the Soviet BOR-60, an experimental 60 MWt fast breeder, which came into operation in December 1968. Since the middle of 1964, however, Soviet engineers in Shevchenko have been building the BN-350 which should reach a capacity of 350 MWe or 1000 MWt. Upon its completion, it will be the largest fast breeder in the world. It will also be the main element of the first large industrial complex in the world to combine an atomic power plant with a desalinisation plant. This complex should be able to produce 150 MW of electrical power as well as 30 million gallons of fresh water per day. The Soviet plan to build an even bigger fast breeder in Beloyarsk, the BN-600, which is to have a capacity of 600 MWe or 1430 MWt. The only fast reactor which the Americans plan to build in the near future is the 400 MWt Fast Flux Test Facility. It ought to be completed by 1973.

The Soviet Union appears to be leading the way in the construction of hydro-electric power stations. The Bratsk plant on the Angara river in East Siberia has a capacity of 4100 MW-more than double that of the largest U. S. hydro-electric plant, the Grand Coulee. The plant at Krasnoyarsk in Siberia, which was almost ready for operation at the end of 1970, will have a capacity of 6000 MW. Its generators, five of which have been in operation since 1968, have a capacity of 500 MW each and are among the largest in the world. It is difficult to estimate the extent to which these achievements are due to the Soviet propensity for gigantism.

The Soviets are also ahead in the high-voltage transmission of electrical energy — 300 kilovolts (kV) or more. The problem of the fast transfer of electrical energy over long distances was obviously very acute in the Soviet Union and had to be solved. In 1959, the Russians brought the first 500 kV transmission line in the world into operation and, by the end of 1969, they had at their disposal a 500 kV high tension network of about 9300 miles and a 330 kV network of 7500 miles.

In 1962, a 265-mile, experimental, direct current (DC) transmission line from Volgograd to Donbas was commissioned. It will provide 750 MW and operates at 800 kV. It will serve as an experimental cable for a 1500 kV direct current line which will be 1600 mile long and will stretch from North Kazakhstan to the East European areas of the Soviet Union. With a capacity of 5250 WM, it is so far the world's most ambitious project for the distribution of direct current. It is expected to be operative in 1975.

4. Coal-mining

With a production of about 608 million tons in 1969, the Soviet Union is the leading coal producing country in the world. But its coal-mining industry can hardly be compared to that of the West because of the different physical and geological characteristics of the coal deposits. Where appropriate comparison is possible, however, Soviet technology and equipment appear to be far less advanced than those of Western Europe and North America.

The thin, sloping, and pitching seams which are prevalent in Soviet underground mines preclude the use of the most advanced type of room-and-pillow method of mining commonly used in the U.S. About 85 % of the Soviet Union's deep-mined coal is obtained by the longwall method. The mechanization of longwall operations is relatively high, although the types used are neither as modern, nor as safe, as those used in West Germany or Great Britain. Tunnel boring and perforating equipment required for building access ways to the pit front have only recently started to be mass produced in the Soviet Union.

All enterprises producing coal by the longwall method aim to develop a fully automated, self-advancing, longwall complex unit which mines the coal and conveys it to the mine transport system. At present, Great Britain leads in the developments of units of this type while the Soviet Union is actively trying to make up its considerable lag in this field.

So far as underground coal-mining is concerned, the widest technological gap between East and West is due to the ancillary operations required at the mine surface. The fact that more than one-fifth of the labor force used in Soviet underground mining is engaged primarily in hand labor above ground shows clearly that the Russians are about ten to fifteen years behind the Americans in both mechanization and efficiency of surface work. Only about 70 % of the coal mined underground in the Soviet Union is mechanically loaded (the same percentage as in the U. S. more than twenty years ago) instead of 90 % in the U. S. The same is true of Western Europe where, as in the Soviet Union, labor costs are lower than in the U. S. when compared to capital costs.

In the development and use of modern technology and equipment for strip mining, the Soviet Union is five to ten years behind the United States. It even trails East Germany. One of the main cost factors in strip mining is the removal of overburden. The thriftiest method, used in almost all American opencast works, is the «dumping» method whereby an excavator — a power-shovel or dragline — continually removes and dumps the earth mass. This technique is necessitated by the fact that the coal seams are found at variable depths beneath the earth. In the Soviet Union, only about a third of the overburden is stripped by the direct dumping method, primarily because of the extreme thickness of the overburden at many coal deposits. The dumping method requires giant-size power-shovels and draglines. The largest American shovels and draglines have bucket capacities of up to 200 cubic yards, whereas the biggest Soviet dragline — still in the planning stage — will have a bucket capacity of only 105 cubic yards.

The Soviet Union is five to ten years behind the United States in the manufacture and use of giant-size trucks for hauling coal from the strip pits. The Soviets have yet to develop an equivalent of the efficient high-capacity unit trains which have been specially conceived for the transport of coal. Soviet coal preparation techniques are about ten years behind those of Western Europe and the United States. In 1967, only about 40 % of the entire Soviet coal production was mechanically cleaned — compared to two-thirds in the U. S. This percentage is about that of the U. S. in 1950—1951. Moreover, the existing Russian coal preparation equipment would be considered obsolete in the major coal producing countries of the West. The use of computers for solving technical and administrative problems is still in its initial stage. The Soviet lag in this area is of about five to ten years.

5. Petroleum

In production of crude oil and natural gas, and in refining capacity, the Soviet Union ranks second to the United States.

Exploitation of the relatively accessible and highly productive reserves which have been major sources of petroleum since World War II has not required the advanced technology and equipment employed by Western oil companies. In addition, the requirement of Soviet economy for high-octane gasolines and other high-quality petroleum products has not been sufficient to command large-scale investements in secondary refining facilities. Consequently, Soviet progress is lagging in seismology, deep drilling, and offshore operations, as well as in the design and engineering of oil and gas producing equipment. However, the Soviets are ahead in the use of water-flooding to maintain the pressure of reservoirs, and in the use of petroleum and natural gas pipelines of a very large diameter.

In oil exploration methods, particularly those requiring seismographical techniques, as well as in the ability to map deep drilling prospects, the Soviet Union is about ten years behind the United States. Gravity and magnetic readings — used to delimit areas suitable for seismographical prospecting — lack the precision of American gravity meters. The inferior quality of Soviet geophones and seismic cables precludes efficient reception and transmission of low frequency signals which reflect earth structures at great depths. The lack of computers and corresponding software prevents automatic processing of seismic data, display of variable density cross sections, and seismographic superimposition or integration of seismograms. Since 1963, the use of computers in seismographic procedures has revolutionized deep exploration for petroleum in the United States.

Today, about 85 % of all Soviet oil and gas wells are operated by the turbodrill method which is particularly effective in shallow, hard rock formations found in the Ural and Volga areas. But this method is of limited efficiency for drilling in the deep, soft rock strata found elsewhere in the country from which most future increases in production must come.

In the U. S., rotary drilling is used in 99 % of cases. It is much more efficient than turbodrilling in softer rock formations, at depths of over 6500 feet. Now that the Soviets must drill for oil where turbodrills cannot be used, they are increasingly forced to import the necessary technology from the West: rotary tools, tricone and diamond drill bits, high-pressure mud pumps, blowout preventers, high-quality drill pipe and cementing equipment.

Soviet production methods are very close to Western ones, with one important exception: from the outset of primary production, Soviet technicians begin water flooding inside new fields in order to maintain reservoir pressure. In the U. S., water flooding is used as a secondary recovery technique and is restricted to the outer edges of old fields where the primary reservoir drive has been exhausted. The Soviet method increases the share of reserves ultimately recovered from high-yield flowing wells and results in the drilling of a smaller number of wells. But it has also lead to early encroachment of water into some productive wells.

Soviet off-shore technology has barely started to develop and is more than ten years behind that of most Western countries. Oil wells 130 feet deep, off the Caspian Sea, could until recently only be reached by directional drilling from onshore locations or by atrificial islands linked to the mainland by trestle-supported railways. At least half-a-dozen mobile offshore platforms are required to explore these offshore deposits which Soviet geologists believe to be extensive. Two such installations are being built in the Soviet Union while a third is being imported from the Netherlands. The Soviet installations will make it possible to drill 6500 deep in 65 feet of water. Among the several hundred offshore platforms of this type existing in the U. S., several can reach a depth of 20 000 feet in close to 1000 feet of water.

The Soviet use the biggest pipelines in the world for the transport of crude oil and natural gas, but some of their components must be imported from West Germany. Automation of the pipeline system is less advanced than in the United States. Pipelines with 48" and 56" in diameter are now being laid in Russia, while the biggest U. S. lines have a diameter of 42". Soviet planners expect to have pipelines with diametres of 80" and 100". But some of the ancillary units built into the Soviet pipeline network do not always correspond to the size of the pipelines. For example, the undersized valves of the 40" gas pipeline connecting Central Asia with the Ural region have reduced capacity by 10 %. Soviet gas pipelines usually operate at lower pressures and have less throughput capacity than American pipelines because of weaker pipes, and because of the lower number and inferior capacity of Soviet compressor stations.

No new oil refinery appears to have been built in the Soviet Union since 1961. Although most of the refining methods developed in the West are used by the Soviets, their experience with some of them is nevertheless very limited. Secondary refinery capacity of the Soviet Union, i. e. catalytic cracking, catalytic reforming, hydro-cracking, hydrogen treating, and alkylation, corresponds to only 20 % of primary crude oil charge capacity. In the U. S., due to the importance of automotive industry and its requirement for high-octane gasoline, secondary petroleum capacity is greater than primary capacity. Such secondary refineries are essential to improve product quality and product mix.

In recent years, the Soviets have brought into operation a catalytic reforming process using platinum catalysts. This method has been used in most Western countries since the mid-fifties. The Soviet Union is also pursuing research into zeolite catalysts to increase yields of gasoline, although it is not known whether these catalysts are actually in use.

With the planned increase in crude oil and natural gas requirements, the fast increasing demand for higher-octane gasoline as well as for high-quality and sulphur-free petroleum products, Soviet industry is confronted with many problems. Since oil wells close to industrial centers are drying up, more distant sources of petroleum must be found. An acute transportation problem has arisen along with the problem of drilling deeper, for which improved drilling methods and equipment must be developed. In addition, new refineries, both with primary and secondary capacity, must be built. The Soviet investment potential will undoubtedly be subject to extremely heavy demands in the near future.

6. The Chemical industry

From an absolute view-point, the Soviet chemical industry is the second most important in the world. But the technology used in the production of many chemicals is at least five years behind that of Western Europe and the United States. Production methods are still obsolete and inadequate, finished products are of inferior quality, production of many new chemicals is insufficient, and the low level of mechanization is obvious. This situation reflects the inappropriate attention given to the development of chemical technology up to the early sixties and the failure to make effective use of available domestic and foreign technology.

The Soviet Union is backward in almost all phases of artificial fertilizer production, from basic research in the development of new production methods and better equipment to the final treatment of artificial fertilizers which purpose is to impart desirable properties. This lag is especially noticeable in the development of concentrated and multinutrient fertilizer and in the production process of ammonia, the main intermediate in manufacturing fertilizers. The United States are four to five years ahead in construction and operation of large ammonia plants of the type which results in substantial cost savings. These plants use more efficient purification processes for raw material and superior centrifugal compressors. As of early 1969, about half the American ammonia production capacity depended on new factories of this type, whereas in the Soviet Union a few such factories became operational for the first time in 1970. With the improved granulating methods used in the West, fertilizers are less apt to lose their nutritive values during transport and storage, and are more easily applied with seed. According to the Plan, in late 1968 the average nutritive value of Soviet artificial fertilizer was 28 % while, in the U. S., the equivalent percentage reached 40 %.

The West also leads the way in petrochemicals. In spite of ten years of development work, the Soviet Union did not produce synthetic glycerine industrially in 1966 whereas 60 % of the American glycerine produced was synthetic. In 1967, almost 90 % of American benzol production came from petrochemical sources as opposed to barely 15 % in the Soviet Union. In 1968, the largest known producer of ethylene in the Soviet

Union had an annual capacity of 60 000 tons, some of the production equipment having been imported from the West. In the U. S., there are several separate ethylene producers with an annual capacity of more than 200 000 tons each.

Soviet efforts to develop more efficient methods for the production of acetylene, acrylonitrile, ammonia, butadiene, ethylene, synthetic glycerine, propylene, and many other chemicals, are hindered by a lack of efficient catalysts for unit operations such as dehydrogenation, and by the inability to produce, in the required quantity and assortment, some types of highly productive pumps, compressors, and other equipment.

In 1967, Soviet plastics production amounted to 18 % of the American production while Soviet artificial fiber production was 30 % of the American. Such production gaps can be explained by the Soviet failure to develop a progressive technology. According to specialists, the Soviet lag is already obvious if one compares U. S. and Soviet methods for the production of polyester, acrylic fibers, butadien styrene, and polybutadiene rubber, as well as synthetic resins such as polyethylene and polyvinyl chloride.

The continued use of obsolete technology is responsible for the inferior quality of some Soviet synthetic materials. The durability of many Soviet synthetic products is only half that of comparable products in the West. This not only indicates technological shortcomings in the production of synthetic rubber, but a lack of high quality stabilizers and additives.

The gaps in Soviet technology, which became obvious early in the sixties, required the importation of entire factory installations and technical know-how which, from 1958 to 1967, cost the equivalent of five billion Swiss francs and were paid with funds originally allocated to the production of synthetic materials and agricultural chemicals. These factory installations were more modern than the Russian ones, but because of Soviet inefficiency in building and operating them, the purchased technology failed to provide the anticipated benefits.

Several significant conclusion on the state of Soviet economy can be drawn from the technological export program for developing countries within the framework of Soviet technical assistance. Chemical production plants built by the Soviets in India (like the refineries previously erected) required an extremely long construction period and are not operating efficiently.

Planning specifications are chronically ignored. As produced in a Soviet-built plant, streptomycin was expected to cost 67 rupees per kilo. Production costs in the Soviet Union itself amounted to 450 rupees. The cheapest non-Soviet source was able to deliver this product to India at 200 rupees. And the actual cost of streptomycin production, once the Soviet factory became operative, was 367 rupees.

7. Metallurgy

Soviet technology is far behind that of the West in the extraction of metal ores, even though modern methods such as mining underwater and in coastal areas have been developed to suit special Soviet conditions. But Soviet mines use obsolete trucks with a load capacity varying from 12 to 25 tons and with a limited range, whereas Western trucks have a maximum load capacity ranging from 70 to 100. The technical level of Soviet ore crushing and processing installations is not up to Western standards.

The same criticism applies to metallurgical technology in which the Soviets have made notable progress, albeit in certain sectors only. Soviet blast furnace technology is the most advanced in the world. The largest blast furnaces were built by the Russians who have developed modern operation methods as, for instance, an efficient preparation of the blast furnace charge by sintering iron ore concentrates. However, the Soviet Union lags noticeably in the use of the latest and most rational pelletizing of fine iron ore concentrates which is widespread in the West. In 1968, Soviet pellet production was of about three million tons, compared with 50 million tons in the United States.

The Soviet Union has built the largest open hearth furnaces in the world to boost its steel production. But the more economic converter process which is increasingly used in the West has barely been introduced. In 1968, Soviet production of oxygen converter steel amounted to 12 % of total steel production, compared with 25 % in Western Europe, 37 % in the U. S., and 74 % in Japan. Although the Soviet Union was ahead in the development of continuous casting, only three per cent of its steel is produced by this technological process which became more widely used in the West than in the Soviet Union. Moscow's central economic planning has been so inflexible, even at plant level, that widespread adoption of new technological methods is usually slow.

So far as metallurgy is concerned, the widest technological gaps between East and West can be found in rollig and finishing. Not only are many Soviet installations obsolete and inefficient by Western standards, but the Soviet Union has also unexplicably failed to supply its high capacity of steel production with appropriate rolling and finishing facilities. It particularly lacks modern cold rolling mills and galvanizing lines. These deficiencies result in a poor assortment of steel products and prevent a much-needed price decrease. For example, the failure to produce adequate quantities of grain-oriented electrical sheet forces the electric power industry to use hot rolled silicon sheet which is less efficient and raises the cost of power transmission. Most Soviet tinplate is produced by the obsolete hot-dip process, whereas in the West the considerably cheaper electrolytic process is in general use.

The Soviet aluminium industry is second to that of the United States and has been actively developed within the last few years. Modern smelters have been built; they are comparable in size and operating efficiency to the best in use in the West. Electrolytic cells found in the most modern Soviet factories operate at 150 000 amperes as opposed to only 120 000 amperes in the newest U. S. factories. On the other hand, the technology used in the production of consumer goods such as aluminium foil and kitchen wares is fully outdated. The continued use of obsolete rolling mills and other old-fashioned installations is reflected in the inferior quality of most products.

The Soviets have recently built a number of plants with technical specifications comparable to Western ones for the production of the other main non-ferrous metals: copper, lead, and zinc. But, on the average, technology is outdated: most factories are obsolete and inefficient. Many years after the West, the Soviet Union is only now beginning to introduce byproduct recovery of sulphuric acid at non-ferrous metals factories; it also lags in the development of methods for the leaching with acid of material in copper waste dumps and the flotation processing of copper oxide ores, both of which processes account for an important part of American copper production.

On the other hand, the Soviet Union is ahead in the production and development of titanium. Soviet technology for the production of titanium alloys is comparable to that of Great Britain and that of the United States. It has produced some of the world's largest titanium forgings for aircraft.

While the Soviet Union has achieved considerable progress in metallurgical research, the practical difficulties which are inescapably bound to the centralized planning system have often kept it from solving the problems involved in translating research results into suitable production technologies. The Russians, for example, have much less experience than the Americans in vacuum metallurgy techniques and have had to import electron beam furnaces from East Germany. However, the Soviet Union holds the lead in the development and use of the electroslag remelting technique which can often be used as a substitute for more traditional vacuum processes; it is backward in advanced rolling methods; particularly when specialized equipment, such as Sendzimir mills, is required.

Although the Soviet Union trails the United States in all general sectors of modern metallurgical techniques, it has nevertheless been able to produce the metals and alloys specifically required by its military and strategic needs. For such priority customers, the Soviets have been able to produce a wide range of high-strength and stainless steels, as well as precipitation hardening steels. In production technology for superalloys, the Soviet Union has reached the same development level as the U. S. and has given top priority to the development of high-temperature, corrosion-resistant metals such as tantalum, niobium, tungsten, molybdenum, rhenium, and zirconium.

8. Machine tools

Although the Soviet Union is the world's largest producer of machine tools, its product mix is heavily weighted with all-purpose machines. But almost all categories of Western machinery equals or surpasses Soviet products in efficiency, durability and accuracy. The average age of Soviet machine tool inventory is considerably younger than that of the United States because of the high rate of Soviet production. Due to the large proportion of all-purpose machines, the technological composition of the Soviet stock is, however, less advanced than that of the United States. This explains why the Soviet press is often critical of this outdated technology and even of the performance of new machines.

The Soviet Union lies way behind the United States in the use of numerically controlled machine tools. The Americans are manufacturing numerically controlled machines equipped with continuous path control on five axes and with automatic tool changing devices; the Soviets only have point-to-point control to two or three axes without automatic tool changing. In the Soviet Union, production of numerically controlled machine tools is only one per cent of the value of total machine tool production, compared to 20 % in the U. S. While the Soviets restrict the use of such machinery in the space industry, the Americans are using them widely in machine factories.

One of these American-made, numerically controlled machine tools is an automatic-transfer machine capable of machine-finishing an engine block, in-line or V-type, according to a numerical program. It combines a high level of automation with the versatility to handle a wide assortment of products. The Soviets are still years away from reaching such a degree of automation and operation control. They have built automatic-transfer machines for industries with high volume production, the automotive and tractor industries for example, but actual production is so limited and delays for delivery so extended that, when large investments are required for factory installations, it resorts to sizeable importations from the free world, such as was the case for the Tol'yatti automobile plant.

The purchase of gear-cutting equipment for the manufacture of rear axle gear at Tol'yatti illustrates the kind of problems which arise in the Soviet Union because of exagerated lead-time. It also shows the technological gap the Soviet Union is building into new plants. Thirty five million Swiss francs worth of equipment was delivered to the Soviets by the American Gleason Works and presumably installed in 1970. However, it will not be operational until 1972. Meanwhile, Gleason is now selling new machinery for cutting bevel drive gears at a cost of barely two million Swiss francs. These machines replaces the five roughing cutters and the ten finishing cutters which were sold for 3,5 million Swiss francs. They are expected to be seven times more productive than the older models and they require less than half the floor space.

The Soviet Union is leading in the fields of electro-discharge machining (EDM) and ultrasonic machining: its production is nearl 50 % of the total world output. On the other hand, the U.S. is ahead of the Soviet Union in the development of electro-chemical (ECM) and electronbeam machining and welding, both processes being of significant importance in space industries.

The Soviet use fewer metal forming machines than metal cutting machinery. Consequently, the waste of steel and non-ferrous mill products is uneconomically high. Nevertheless, the Soviets have developed leading technologies for metal moulding — albeit in isolated cases — such as the unique Soviet process for rolling gears and shafts from heated steel billets at a much higher rate than cutting tools can achieve. The two largest forging presses (75 000 tons each) in the world are in the Soviet Union. They produce oversized working parts for large high-performance and supersonic aircraft. The largest forging press currently in use in the United States has a capacity of only 54 000 tons.

An extremely significant experience made by the Russians in India has shown that the Soviet machine-tool industry is also plagued by serious deficiencies. In mid-1956, the Soviets began to advise the Indians on the development of an indigenous machine-tool industry. Within the scope of this cooperation, a project was worked out in 1957 for the construction of a factory which was to manufacture heavy machine-tools for the coal industry. In February 1960, plans were finalized and the required contracts between India and the Soviet Union were signed. However, due to the insufficient and — mostly — badly delayed Soviet delivery of equipment, 11 years after the approval of the plans this plant reached a production of only about 5000 tons, instead of a planned capacity of 45 000 tons per year. Half-a-billion rupees have already been invested in this enterprise. After an exhaustive and careful investigation, a committee of the Indian House of the People has recommended to shut down the factory to avoid further losses. Even though, for propaganda reasons, the Soviet Union would have liked to see the successful completion of this project to which its prestige remains attached, it has obviously grossly overestimated its capacity.

9. Automotive industry

The Soviet automotive industry was developed in the late twenties and early thirties with the technical aid of American automobile companies. In 1968, it manufactured approximately 480 000 trucks (505 000 in 1969) and 280 000 passenger cars (295 000 in 1969), compared to about 1,9 million trucks and 8,8 million passenger cars produced in the U. S. during the same year. Production outputs notwithstanding, the inverse ratio of Soviet and U. S. truck-car productions once again emphasizes the nature of Communist economy compared to that of the United States: the first is power-oriented; the second is a consumer's economy.

Soviet engineers have developed a small assortment of special body styles for trucks, such as dump bodies, fire apparatus, tank wagons, and standard vans. Specialized truck bodies, such as those for mechanical refrigeration, transit cement mixing, trash removal, powerline maintenance, furniture moving, etc., are only built in small numbers — if at all.

From 1945 to 1963, automotive industry investments were concentrated on the production of 4 and $4^1/2$ ton trucks in the ZIL Moscow plant, and on the production of $2^1/2$ ton trucks in the GAZ plant at Gorkiy. Both ZIL and GAZ models were essentially copies of World War II, U. S. made vehicles which were then delivered to the Soviets within the scope of military assistance. ZIL and GAZ trucks, in production since 1946, have recently been replaced by newer models, but the $2^1/2$ ton GAZ truck is still built today.

The new models display an array of up-to-date features: air or vacuum boosted brakes, power steering, oil coolers, radiator shutters (for improved temperature regulation). Engine designs are copied from Western engines and include substantial improvements: interchangeable cylinder liners, sodium filling of exhaust valves, and chromium plating of upper compression rings. Most of them are reasonably efficient V-8 engines. However, considering their piston displacement, they develop less horsepower than equivalent Western engines because of the low compression ratios required by the octane-poor Soviet gasoline. The Soviet octane contents are about 20 % below Western ones; compression ratios used on Soviet trucks vary from 6:1 to 6,5:1, compared to 7,5:1 and 8,5:1 in the West.

Soviet trucks have a smaller payload than Western trucks of comparable weight and of similar tire size. The ZIL 130, one of the most modern trucks built in the Soviet Union, can transport a load of four to five tons, depending on road conditions, whereas an American truck of about the same gross vehicle weight (truck plus cargo) carries more than seven tons. The smaller payload of Soviet trucks is not only due to the inferior quality of metals used in the manufacture of chassis and axles, but also to the poor condition of Soviet roads which contribute to the comparatively fast wear and tear of Soviet-made trucks. The weight payload ratio of the new dump trucks (25 tons and more) have been improved but, in most cases, it still fails to match that of Western trucks of this type.

Until a few years ago, Soviet production of passenger cars had been neglected in order to better fulfil the needs of the power-oriented State economy. Since then, an expansion program has been put into effect; it is expected to boost the yearly car production from approximately 250 000 units in 1967 to over one million in 1973, a forecast which seems rather over-optimistic considering that barely 280 000 cars came off the Soviet assembly lines in 1969.

There are basically three different types of passenger cars manufactured in the Soviet Union: the tiny Zaporozhets (comparable to the Fiat 600), the small four-seater Moskvich (similar to the Opel Kadett), and the medium-sized Volga (rather like U. S. compact cars of the Chevy Nova or Rambler American type). A small number of GAZ Chaika sedans and ZIL 111 limousines are built, practically by hand; they are powered by six and eight cylinder engines respectively. Otherwise, all Soviet passenger cars are equiped with four cylinder engines which, however, develop less horsepower than comparable Western engines. In spite of considerable efforts, the Soviet attempt to set foot commercially in the West and to promote the sale of their cars has been a total failure, at least until now.

Soviet automobiles are built to withstand the severe Russian winter weather as well as the more than mediocre Soviet roads.

Due to their stiff suspension systems, their ride is uncomfortable while the noise and vibrations emanating from their engines simply do not comply with Western requirements.

Soviet truck drivers complain about the poor quality of interior equipment such as window and door sealings, upholstery, about the insufficient isolation from noise and heat, and about the poor weather resistance of body paints. The inferior quality of Soviet sheet metal (processed by cold lamination) requires heavy bodies and accounts for a poor surface finish.

Compared to Western standards, the technological level of the Soviet automotive industry as a whole is just as obsolete as the product mix. A trade expert describes the Soviet automotive industry as «incredibly outdated and ineffective» by Western standards. The Soviets are relying on imported plans and equipment in order at least to narrow the gap separating their industry from that of the West. Following the signature of a contract with Fiat of Italy, a huge automobile plant has been built at Tol'yatti (formerly Stavropol) on the Volga. The French Renault company offers technical help and provides new installations to the Moskvich Works to boost their production rate. The purchase by the Soviets of entire installations capable of a yearly production of 180 000 trucks has been under consideration for some time. Negotiations with the American Ford Motor Company collapsed when Ford realized that the installation of an economically sound enterprise in the Soviet Union was fraught with enormous and nearly unsurmountable difficulties. Nor could the Americans overlook Fiat's unfortunate experiences in this task. The rumor according to which the negociations broke down under pressure exerted by the U. S. government, which supposedly feared the shipment of Soviet-made Ford trucks to Vietnam, seems to have been propagated by Moscow. Similar negociations, first with the Japanese, then with Mercedes of West-Germany, also failed to bring any results. Whether the latest Soviet attempt (with the French Régie Renault) will eventually materialize into a working agreement still remains to be seen.

Since 1960, the Soviet Union has been the top tractor producing country in the world. Over 405 000 units came off the assembly lines in 1967 (442 000 in 1969), compared to 260 000 in the U. S. Despite a few technical improvements, Soviet tractors are still inferior to Western models in many respects:

power-to-weight ratio, transmission efficiency, dependability and durability, as well as ease of operation and upkeep. Soviet tractors are too heavy: manufacturers try to make up for the inferior quality of Soviet metal (partly caused by deficient quality control in metal casting) by a weight increase. The poor reliability and short service life results in part from the low quality of even such ordinary items as bolts, welded joints, piston rings, inadequate lubrication, insufficient dirt protection of bearing components, faulty hardening of wear surfaces. The acute lack of spare parts is an additional shortcoming: the Soviet industry does not provide customer service in compliance with Western requirements.

The transmission systems of Soviet tractors are much less efficient than those of Western models. Drawbar horsepower of an average Soviet tractor ranges from 60 to 65 % of the engine horsepower, compared to 90 % for an American tractor. This explains why fuel consumption is high compared to Western figures. Although modern features (copied from Western models) such as four-wheel drive and power-steering for wheeled tractors, and automatic transmission for wheeled and tracted tractors, are standard equipment on some Soviet vehicles, they do not match the most recent technical developments. Moreover, Soviet machinery, with its growing mechanization and automation, is increasingly prone to repairs.

The Soviet tractor industry does not have at its disposal the know-how and the factory installations required for the production of a vehicle comparable to the American caterpillar D-9G which has been successfully introduced on mining and building sites. Nor has it yet developed the necessary engines and powershift transmissions. The Soviet Union has imported a number of U. S. made D-9 truck-tractors for its Magadan goldmines where this type of machine is particularly useful to tear open the deep-frozen ground.

10. Aircraft industry

The Soviet aircraft industry is the second largest in the world. The Soviet Union has long stressed research on supersonic and hypersonic flight. Its industry can, consequently, produce fighters and intercepters competitive with other aircraft of this type in the world. Western powers have the edge, however, when it comes to heavy bombers.

Due to frequent engine deficiencies, operating conditions of Soviet transport planes cannot be favorably compared to Western ones. Although the latest types of civilian transport planes now in production are substantially improved compared to preceding models, their operating range, payload, fuel consumption, and engine life are still inferior to those of similar Western aircraft. Interior equipment, especially passenger accomodations, do not meet Western requirements. Extensive comparative tests made in India, and numerous experiments made by foreign airlines flying Soviet-made passenger aircraft, conclusively show that Soviet production in this field is inferior. Soviet planes have turned out to be an economic burden and have been eliminated as quickly as possible, as in Ghana for example. Indonesia has decided not to order any more Soviet-made planes because of past «bitter experiences». Technical instructions were missing when planes were delivered and the availability of indispensable spare-parts could never be guaranteed. Soviet airplanes rather than Western aircraft had been ordered because of Soviet economic aid or because of political pressure from Moscow.

In the Soviet aircraft industry, far too much time is lost between test flights and actual production. The Ilyushin IL-62, the only jet-propelled Soviet airliner comparable to the Boeing 707, the Douglas DC-8, and the British VC-10, flew for the first time in 1963, but was still not in service by mid-1967. The Tupolev TU-134, a Soviet aircraft corresponding to the Douglas DC-9, made its maiden flight in 1963, but actual production of the plane did not start until the beginning of 1968. For comparison purposes, it should be pointed out that the initial series of forty DC-9s were delivered 18 months after the first test-flight of this aircraft.

Insofar as supersonic flight is concerned, Soviet technology is nearly level with that of the West. Experience acquired with the Mach 3XB-70 has provided the United States with a broad technological background for the development of an advanced strategic bomber. Test data obtained from the slower (Mach 2,2) TU-144 supersonic transport (SST), which first flew in December 1968, will bolster Soviet capabilities in this field.

Incidentally, Soviet science evidently has had some «outside help» in developing the TU-144. When the Soviets displayed their new supersonic liner at the Paris air show, late in the spring of 1971, even casual observers were struck by the uncanny similarity between the aircraft's characteristics (overall shape, performance, etc.) and those of the Concorde. Pure coincidence?

In an article published by the Parisian daily «L'Aurore», Peter Hamilton, one of the leading figures in British counter-espionage, has indicated the extent to which the development of the TU-144 is «one of the most obvious examples of industrial espionage». A spy ring led by Herbert Steinbrecher, a West-German, functioned from 1958 until 1964 when it was dismantled. In his confession, Jean-Paul Suppert, Steinbrecher's main collaborator, has revealed that an amazingly large amount of secret data on the Concorde had been relayed to Moscow. Steinbrecher was sentenced to 12 years of imprisonment. But his organisation was soon to be replaced by another headed by Sergey Pavlov, director of the Paris office of Aeroflot (the Soviet airline). A short time later, in February 1965, Pavlov was arrested in Paris as he was about to transmit confidential informations on the metal components which were to be used in the construction of Concorde's fuselage. He was immediately expelled from France.

The Soviets then resorted to the use of two brothers, Stephan and Sarady Grigorsky, provided by the Czechoslovak secret service. They were both arrested — one year after Pavlov — and sentenced respectively to eight and four years of prison.

On December 31, 1968, however, two months before the Concorde, the TU-144 made its first test-flight thus proving that, in spite of the risks involved, Soviet espionage had accomplished its task diligently and successfully.

Looking at another sector of the aircraft industry, it appears that the Soviet Union holds the lead in the development of rotor systems for giant helicopters, as well as in some branches of helicopter industry: rear ramp loading, electrical bonding on external controls, ice detector systems, deicing of rotor blades, automatic pilot, stubwing, oxygen system, blade tip lights. On the other hand, the United States are substantially ahead in the design and development of fast tactical helicopters and associated weapon systems, as well as in rigid rotor and compound helicopters.

11. Electronics

The soviet electronics industry is officially classified as a defense industry. It is part of the politically relevant power sector of the economy and shares with the missile, nuclear, and other strategic industries a priority claim to Soviet economic ressources. Most of its output is defense-related. Isolated from the consumer economy, the power economy is provided with the best workers and top priority in capital investment.

At the time of Stalin's death in 1953, the electronics industry was rather neglected partly because of the dogmatic ideologists resistance against cybernetics. It is only later that its value as a power factor in politics was recognized by the Soviets who developed an electronics industry in a relatively short time. Today, the Soviet Union ranks second to the United States in this field. The successful launching of the first artificial satellite in October 1957 was the first testimony of Soviet achievements: it could not have taken place without first-rate computers. Moreover, it indicated that the Soviet Union had developed a superior fuel with a high propulsion capacity. The weight capacity of Soviet satellites was greater than that of the Americans and the Soviet Union was to temporarily hold the lead in the satellite race.

Nowadays, however, the technological level of Soviet electronic equipment is inferior to its U. S. counterpart. For over ten years, American electronic equipment has been transistorized — the use of transistors and semi-conductor diodes included. In the Soviet Union, transistors have only been widely used in electronics since 1967 approximately.

The difference in capacity is mainly due to the fact that semi-conductor components are used for different purposes. The U. S. manufactures mainly silicon devices, using epitaxial planar production methods, while the Soviet Union produces mostly germanium transistors and only recently appears to have been able to manufacture silicum planar units industrially. Because of the inherently superior indices of silicon planar devices, American electronic equipment tends to exceed its Soviet counterpart in all important operational parameters.

So far as military electronics are concerned, the Soviet Union still uses equipment containing hybrid packages combining transistors and obsolete electron tubes. In top priority military areas, such as missile/guidance and control systems, as well as strategic early warning radar systems, the Soviet Union has achieved a rough parity with the United States in terms of equipment performance. But Soviet equipment tends to be larger and heavier, less transportable, more difficult to maintain, and less reliable than similar U. S. equipment.

The gap in component technology is widening. In the U. S., transistors are rapidly being replaced by integrated circuits which are largely experimental in the Soviet Union. In many fields, such as computers, electronic instruments, telephone equipment, television (especially color TV), the Soviet Union is far behind the United States. The gap in micro-electronics can be estimated at about four years.

Western computers — and in particular the American models — are far superior to those made by the Soviets in reliability and in important operational parameters; speed, memory size, and multiple access capability. The latest American equipment uses mainly integrated circuits which improve working capacity, allow for a more compact size of computers and lower manufacturing costs; Soviet computers in current production are based on transistor technology.

The gap between the Soviet and the U. S. computer technology is increasing. The Americans are about to launch the fourth generation of computers, based on large-scale integration and characterized by greater speed and reliability. A modern Soviet computer like the BESM-6 is capable of handling one million operations per second, compared to the six million effected by IBM models. Up to now, only a handful of BESM-6 computers are operational although the prototype first appeared in 1965.

Details about the number of computers available in Communist countries are not readily available. According to the Hungarian, «Figyelö» (October 1969), there were in 1967 200 computers per million inhabitants in the U. S., 78 in Switzerland, 50 in the Common Market countries, and only 12 in the Soviet Union. At that time, there were about 40 000 computers operating in the U. S., about 11 000 in the non-Communist European states, 2800 in the Soviet Union, and about 3400 in all the Comecon states. Today, the Soviet Union should have about 4000 computers, while the East European states under its influence, including Yugoslavia, have another 800, out of which only about 250 are manufactured at home, 430 have been imported from the West, and only 120 come from the Soviet Union — a significant indication on East European preference and on Soviet achievements in that field.

The Soviet Union can scarcely close the existing gap without substantial Western aid. This is why the Soviets attempted in 1969 to obtain a manufacturing license from a British computer firm which uses American technology. The Tunis newspaper, «L'Action», reported on June 25, 1970, that a third generation U. S. computer, exported to India, had mysteriously turned up in the Soviet Union where it was taken apart and closely examined with intent to copy it.

The Soviet Union also trails the West in the technology of industrial and scientific instrumentation. The oscilloscope is typical of technology in the field of electronic equipment: flexibility band width is the most important single criterion for complexity and overall capability. Oscilloscopes capable of sensing radio frequencies above 30 million cycles per second are in very short supply in the Soviet Union, whereas instruments with capabilities of 150 million cycles per second are quite common in the U. S. For exacting scientific research, the Soviets have to import from the West such instruments as electron microscopes and nuclear magnet resonance spectrometers.

The Soviet Union is several years behind the United States in the technology of commercial communications. With considerable help from Czechoslovakia, the Soviet Union was only recently able to develop crossbar exchanges of one-thousand line capacity, whereas in the U. S. crossbar exchanges of several thousand lines have been commercially available for many years. In the technology of carrier systems (multiplexing) for cable and radio relay communications, the capacity of American systems commercially available is at least ten times that of the systems produced in the Soviet Union.

Color television is a striking example of the backwardness of Soviet technology when applied to the consumer area. Although the Soviets had already developed prototype color television tubes in 1959, they have been technologically unable to manufacture them on a large scale. Consequently, plans to commercially develop color TV have been delayed for several years. The Soviet Union has finally had to obtain the necessary know-how for industrial production from the U. S. in order to begin mass producing color TV sets in the current year.

The Soviet Union is 3 to 5 years behind in communications satellite technology. In 1958, the U. S. Army's Score was the first to transmit pre-recorded messages. In the early sixties, the U. S. followed up this early success with the Courier, Telstar, Relay and Syncom satellites, which paved the way for the successful U. S. launching of Early Bird in April 1965. It was the first satellite in the world to be deployed operationally and used regularly for commercial communications. During the same month, the Soviets successfully launched a satellite which was also specifically designed as a news relay station. They called it Molniya, or lightning, and considered it experimental until 1967.

Molniya satellites do not seem to have satisfactory active lifetimes, probably because of their pronouncedly elliptical orbit which has the advantage of covering the territory of the Soviet Union more efficiently. But because the satellite repeatedly passes through the Van Allen radiation belts, and because it requires a constant correction of the lateral drift inherent to an elliptical orbit, the latter is hard on spacecraft components. Since 1965, the Soviets have orbited at least 11 Molniya satellites. It thus implies that many still in orbit are no longer operative. Early Bird, on the other hand, was still functioning satisfactorily when, at the beginning of 1969, it was pulled out of active duty. The three Intelsat-II satellites which were put into stationary orbit by the U. S. in 1967 are also still fully operational.

On-board transmitter power of the Molniya satellites is greater than that of any American satellite. But its traffic-handling capacity is apparently limited to only 60 two-way telephone channels compared to the 240 channels available in Early Bird and the Intelsat-II series, while the two Intelsat-III satellites orbited in 1969 have an operating capacity of 1200 channels. The number of channels available in Soviet comsats appears to have remained static since 1965, whereas American technological progress has led to their five-fold increase in the same period.

During the last three years, the Soviet Union has made fast progress in developing the ground segment of its comsat program.

Until 1967, the only two ground stations known to handle Molniya transmissions were in Moscow and in Vladivostok. In November 1967 however, a network of more than twenty so-called Orbita ground stations were put into operation, each capable of receiving one TV channel relayed from Moscow via Molniya. But, in contrast to the main stations in Moscow and Vladivostok, none of the Orbita stations is currently able to receive telephone and telegraph traffic, or has a ground-to-satellite transmission capability. The United States have six Intelsat ground stations in operation on home ground and American technology is directly, or indirectly, responsible for most of the 16 other Intelsat stations operating today in other countries. All Intelsat stations have full range capabilities — that is, they can transmit and receive all types of communications.

It is expected that the Soviets will soon substantially improve their comsat technology, as compared to present accomplishments, and that in should soon reach greater sophistication. There are indications that the Soviet Union has put — or is about to put — a comsat into equatorial synchronous orbit. Future Soviet comsats will almost certainly be equipped with a larger number of transmitting and receiving channels. If these improvements occur within the next year or two, it will indicate that the technological gap in this field will be narrower — at least temporarily. But American technology is far from stationary. The fourth generation of Intelsat satellites is designed for 5000 to 6000 two-way voice channels, for simultaneous access with a large number of ground stations, and for a useful lifetime of seven years. If, as it is planned, the Intelsat-IV series is soon brought into operation, the United States will then have a three-year advantage over the Soviet Union in comsat technology. The Americans are bound to retain their lead in the foreseeable future.

12. Consumer goods

Production technology in the Soviet consumer goods industry is uneven, but on average extremely outdated, due to the priority given to the strategically much more important heavy industry. The immense efforts of the Soviet people are forceably directed towards strengthening state power rather than to increasing the prosperity of the individual. But there are exceptions: archaic textile works stand side by side with the most modern bread factories.

The typical Soviet bread factory operates with a continuous flow process: the ingredients are mixed in huge vats on the top floor of a multistory building. While the dough moves slowly downwards, many different bread products are formed, baked, unpacked on the ground floor, and loaded on to special vehicles for direct delivery to the distribution centers. The automation level is high and quality control is strict. Similar mass production methods are not as common in the West.

The technological level of the Soviet food industry is, otherwise, 20 to 25 years behind that of the United States. Some of the better Soviet equipment now in production is merely a copy of equipment used in America during the thirties and does not apply the advanced methods developed in Western Europe and even Eastern Germany. Deep freeze units are extremely rare in Soviet households and very little fresh frozen produce and meats are processed in the Soviet Union. The most prevalent way of preserving food is that of canning in glass jars, an operation done by the consumer himself. Equipment for the automatic packing of liquid dairy products in paper containers, as well as for automatically wrapping and packaging butter and cheese, is practically non-existent.

The equipment of Soviet textile mills is as much as 25 to 30 years older than that of Western plants. Attempts are being made to replace old machinery with new units produced in the Soviet Union. But even the latest Soviet machines offer little improvement over those produced fifty years ago. The manufacture of textiles from synthetic fiber is entirely dependent on imported machinery. The Soviet textile industry lacks modern finishing equipment; the quality of the finished product is very low compared with Western standards. Pre-shrinking machinery is hardly available. Only now are first steps being taken for steam-processing of the more expensive woolen products. Machinery for the manufacture of wrinkle-free, no-iron, and permanent-crease materials is not yet in production. There are very few bleaching installations: most Soviet cotton products are dyed without first being bleached, which makes them unattractive to the eye. All in all, it takes about twice as much labor to produce a ton of cotton fabric in the Soviet Union than in the U.S. The simple fact that Soviet thread breaks more easily entails a 20 % deficiency in work productivity in Soviet textile industry as compared to the American.

According to Soviet data, less than 65 % of work operations in the Soviet shoe industry are mechanized. A third of the equipment is considered as obsolete. Even the latest type of Soviet machinery is well below world standards. The technology of the Soviet clothing industry is geared to the mass production of a narrow selection of simple styles. Compared to its Western counterpart, it is lagging in the same proportion as the textile and shoe industries.

With respect to consumer durables, household appliances produced in the Soviet Union are of inferior quality, old-fashioned, and inefficient. Most of them are comparable to pre-World War II Western models.

Appliances and other housewares are mostly by-products of heavy machinery and aircraft industries. Radio and television sets are aso manufactured with obsolete production methods compared to those used in the West.

Soviet retail trade, which has always been at a disadvantage, is hardly comparable to that of the West. According to Soviet data, 88 % of all retail activities are done by hand. True to this is the time-honored use of the abacus which is only slowly being replaced with the adding machine or the cash register.

For comparison purposes, in 1964, a worker in a Soviet match factory was able to process about 15 000 cubic feet of wood while an American worker could process from 25 000 to 31 000 cubic feet.

The gap is even greater in the paper industry. The amount of cellulose paper or carton produced by a single Soviet worker is 20 to 25 % below that of an American, and 25 to 30 % below that of a Finnish worker.

The gap in agricultural work productivity is growing at an increasing rate to the disadvantage of the Soviet Union. The Soviet index for agricultural work productivity rose from 100 in 1940 to 270 in 1969, but the equivalent American index for the same period rose from 100 to 437, bearing in mind that, in 1940 already, American work productivity was higher than that of the Soviet Union.

13. Conclusions

This comparison by sector clearly shows the great technological gap between the Soviet Union and the United Staates.

This gap is general, but it is at its widest in the consumer sectors of the economy and at its narrowest in sectors affected by power political considerations. The contradiction between consumer economy and power economy is here obvious.

The Soviet Union cannot bridge the gap without Western help. If popular pressure to expand the consumer goods sector increases, the Soviets will find it extremely difficult to keep the power economy gap as small as it is today.

Without a doubt, progress was made: remarkable Soviet achievements have come about in several industrial fields. Still, they can hardly be called miraculous, after more than fifty years of Communist domination. What is actually more amazing is that, on the whole, this progress has been so modest.

The policy of burdening the economy with uneconomic planning considerations, based entirely on power politics, has prevented greater improvement and will continue to be detrimental, since it cannot possibly provide a sound working system.

The example of Japan is significant in this respect. Japan lost the war in 1945 instead of winning it; it had to pay reparations instead of receiving them; it is poor rather than rich in raw materials. Yet, within barely 25 years, Japan has been able to achieve an impressive economic development for which the free market economy is largely responsible. Taiwan and South Korea, like Japan and West Germany, have also performed «economic miracles». Conclusions are bound to be drawn from the fact that, so far, «economic miracles» are restricted to countries with a free economy and that developments of this kind have yet to appear in countries with centrally planned economies.

In these countries, short-term foreign trade is very limited and long-term trade is still considerably restricted.

The forecast according to which the Communist countries' proportion of world trade will double or even treble in the near future is hardly realistic. The division of Soviet economy into what has been termed a power economy and a consumer economy implies that, when it comes to foreign trade, the economic potential of these countries is limited by political considerations, while the political potential would seem to be limited by economic considerations.

Peter Sager

Report
from
Vietnam

Berne, 1968

Salvador de Madariaga

On
Freedom

Berne, 1970

Swiss Eastern Institute Press

SOCIAL SCIENCE LIBRARY

Manor Road Building
Manor Road
Oxford OX1 3UQ
Tel. (2)71093 (enquiries and renewals)
http://www.ssl.ox.ac.uk

WITHDRAWN

This is a NORMAL LOAN item.

We will email you a reminder before this item is due.

Please see http://www.ssl.ox.ac.uk/lending.html
for details on:

- loan policies; these are also displayed on the notice boards and in our library guide.

- how to check when your books are due back.

- how to renew your books, including information on the maximum number of renewals.
  Items may be renewed if not reserved by another reader. Items must be renewed before the library closes on the due date.

- level of fines; fines are charged on overdue books.

Please note that this item may be recalled during Term.